Massachusetts Historical Society.

MEMOIR

OF THE

HON. NATHAN APPLETON, LL.D.

G. P A Healy S. A. Schoff

Yours truly
N. Appleton

MEMOIR

OF THE

HON. NATHAN APPLETON, LL.D.

PREPARED AGREEABLY TO A RESOLUTION

OF THE

MASSACHUSETTS HISTORICAL SOCIETY.

BY ROBERT C. WINTHROP.

With an Introduction and Appendix.

BOSTON:
PRINTED BY JOHN WILSON AND SON,
22, SCHOOL STREET.
1861.

CONTENTS.

PAGE.

Proceedings of the Massachusetts Historical Society 1

MEMOIR OF HON. NATHAN APPLETON,
By Hon. Robert C. Winthrop 5

APPENDIX.

Meeting in the Merchants' Exchange 65
Remarks of John A. Lowell, Esq. 65
Remarks of J. T. Stevenson, Esq. 66
Remarks of Hon. Edward Everett 68

Resolutions adopted at a Meeting of the Directors of the Massachusetts Hospital Life-Insurance Company . . . 73

Resolutions adopted at a Meeting of the Merrimack Manufacturing Company 74

Proceedings at a Meeting of the Directors of the Boston Bank . 75

Proceedings at a Meeting of the Proprietors of Stark Mills, with the Remarks of William Amory, Esq. 75

Remarks of Ex-Governor Lincoln at the Annual Meeting of the American Antiquarian Society. 77
Resolutions adopted at the same Meeting 78

MASSACHUSETTS HISTORICAL SOCIETY.

At the stated monthly meeting of this Society, held at their rooms on Thursday, 8th August, 1861, the President (Hon. Robert C. Winthrop) announced the death of the Hon. Nathan Appleton, a Resident Member of the Society, as follows: —

We have been called on so often of late, gentlemen, to notice the departure of those whose names have adorned our Honorary or our Resident rolls, that the language of eulogy may seem to have been almost exhausted. Yet I am sure you would not excuse me, nor could I excuse myself, were I to fail to make some brief allusion this morning to a valued and venerable associate, who died only a day or two after our last monthly meeting.

Lowell, the revered pastor; Shaw, the illustrious jurist; White, the accomplished counsellor and scholar; Bowditch, the faithful conveyancer and genial humorist, whose diligence has illustrated so many title-deeds, and whose wit has illuminated so many title-names; — all these and more have received, in sad succession, our farewell tributes within a few months past. The wise, upright and eminent merchant presents no inferior claim to our respectful remembrance, nor will his name be associated with less distinguished or less valuable services to the community.

Not many men, indeed, have exercised a more important influence among us, during the last half-century, than the late Hon. NATHAN APPLETON. Not many men have done more than he has done, in promoting the interests, and sustaining the institutions, to which New England has owed so much of its prosperity and welfare. No man has done more, by example and by precept, to elevate the standard of mercantile character, and to exhibit the pursuits of commerce in proud association with the highest integrity, liberality, and ability.

The merchants of Boston have already recognized his peculiar claims to their respect, and have paid him a tribute not more honorable to him than to themselves. But he was more than a merchant. As a clear and vigorous writer on financial and commercial questions; as a successful expounder of some of the mysteries of political economy; as a wise and prudent counsellor in the public affairs of the country, as well as in the practical concerns of private life; as a liberal friend to the institutions of religion, education, and charity; as a public-spirited, Christian citizen, of inflexible integrity and independence, — he has earned a reputation quite apart from the enterprise and success of his commercial career.

Few of those whose names, for thirty years past, have been inscribed with his own on the rolls of our Society, have taken a more active and intelligent interest in our pursuits. Few have been more regular in their attendance at our meetings, or more liberal in their contributions to our means.

Tracing back his descent to an early emigrant from the county of Suffolk in England, where his family had been settled for more than two centuries before, he was strongly attracted towards our Colonial history, and was eager to co-operate in whatever could worthily illustrate the Pilgrim or the Puritan character. He was a living illustration of some of the best elements of both.

This is not the occasion for entering into the details of his life and services; but, should the Society concur with the Standing Committee in the resolutions which they have instructed me to submit, there may be an opportunity of pursuing the subject more deliberately hereafter. Let me only add, before offering them, that, on many accounts, I should have been disposed to shrink from the responsibility which they impose on me, had not our lamented friend so far honored me with his confidence as to express the wish, that I would undertake any little memoir of him which might be customary in our collections, — accompanying the expression with some sketches of his life, which will form the largest and best part of whatever I may be able to prepare.

Mr. Winthrop then offered the following resolutions: —

Resolved, That, in the death of the Hon. NATHAN APPLETON, our Society has lost a valued member, a liberal friend, and one whose enterprise and integrity as a merchant, whose ability and accomplishments as a writer, and whose distinguished services as a public man, have rendered his name an ornament to our rolls.

Resolved, That the President be requested to prepare the customary memoir for our next volume of Proceedings.

The Rev. Dr. BLAGDEN paid an eloquent tribute to the memory of Mr. Appleton in seconding the resolutions, which were then unanimously adopted.

MEMOIR

OF

HON. NATHAN APPLETON.

At early dusk on some October or November evening, in the year 1794, a fresh, vigorous, bright-eyed lad, just turned of fifteen, might have been seen alighting from a stage-coach near Quaker Lane,* as it was then called, in the old town of Boston. He had been two days on the road from his home in the town of New Ipswich, in the State of New Hampshire. On the last of the two days, the stage-coach had brought him all the way from Groton in Massachusetts; starting for that purpose early in the morning, stopping at Concord for the passengers to dine, trundling them through Charlestown about the time the evening lamps were lighted, and finishing the whole distance of rather more than thirty miles in season for supper. For his first day's journey, there had been no such eligible and expeditious conveyance. The Boston stage-coach, in those days, went no farther than Groton in that direction. His father's farm-horse, or perhaps that of one of the neighbors,

---

* Now Congress Street.

had served his turn for the first six or seven miles; his little brother of ten years old having followed him as far as Townsend, to ride the horse home again. But from there he had trudged along to Groton on foot, with a bundle-handkerchief in his hand, which contained all the wearing apparel he had, except what was on his back. He was now, on the second evening, at his journey's end. He had reached the destined scene of his labors and of his life; and it may be hoped, that when he laid himself down to rest that night, alone and in a strange place, some bright visions of success in the future may have mingled with his dreams of home, and honored parents, and affectionate brothers and sisters, whom he had left behind him, and may have softened the sadness of that first parting.

At early dawn on the morning of Sunday, the 14th of July, 1861, there died, at his beautiful residence in Beacon Street, — adorned, within, by many choice works of luxury and art, and commanding, without, the lovely scenery of the Mall, the Common, and the rural environs of Boston, — a venerable person of more than fourscore years; a merchant of large enterprise and unsullied integrity; a member of many learned societies; a writer of many able essays on commerce and currency; a wise and prudent counsellor in all private and public affairs; who had served with marked distinction in the legislative halls both of the State and of the Nation, and who had enjoyed through life the esteem, respect, and confidence of the community in which he lived. His funeral, three days afterwards, was attended by a large concourse of his fellow-citizens, and by representative men of all professions and classes. A few hours before the funeral, a public meeting was held at the Exchange, on occasion of his death, at which tributes were paid to his memory by several of our most distinguished merchants and citizens, who all spoke of him as "fit for an example," — as a man whom the young merchants of Boston might well take as their model, and strive to copy. And on the succeeding Sunday, in the pulpit of the church with which he had been long associated, an eloquent occasional discourse concluded with the following words: "A Christian merchant, whose faith is at once his safeguard and his impulse, whose conscience is shown in what he says, and whose heart shines through his deeds, falls behind no example that may claim the praise, or provoke the imitation, of men. When such an one passes on to the eternal world, let those who have beheld his excellence profit by its instruction, and repeat its history." *

As we contemplate in immediate connection, and in immediate contrast, the two scenes which have thus been sketched, we naturally desire to know all that is to be known of the interval between such an opening, and such a close, of one and the same career; and to understand, so far as it may be fathomed, the secret of so signal a success. No details would seem to be too minute or trifling, which might help to illustrate such an example, or to bring it more nearly within the reach of imitation by those to whom it has been so justly com-

* "Religion conducive to Prosperity in this Life;" a sermon preached July 21, 1861, — the Sunday after the funeral of the late Hon. Nathan Appleton, of Boston, — by Ezra S. Gannett, D.D. Boston: 1861. J. H. Eastburn's press.

mended. Fortunately, abundant materials are not wanting for this purpose, from the most authentic source; while the simplicity and unity of the career which they disclose, will allow the portrait to be finished without greatly exceeding the compass of our ordinary memoirs.

NATHAN APPLETON was born in New Ipswich, N.H., on the sixth day of October, 1779; and although his first journey to Boston, in 1794, would seem to indicate that he was a lad of very humble fortunes, he was by no means without advantages of family and education. Few families, indeed, in New England, and not a great many in Old England, can be traced farther back than his own, through a respectable ancestry, and by an unquestioned pedigree. Among the Harleian Manuscripts in the British Museum is found a genealogy reaching back to John Appulton of Great Waldingfield, in the county of Suffolk, who was living there in 1396, and whose funeral monument in the parish church of that village, in 1416, was duly decorated (according to Weever) with "three apples *gules*, leaves and stalks *vert*." Among the descendants of this John Appulton, some of whom were settled in Great and some in Little Waldingfield, — some of whom were connected with knightly families, and at least one of whom bore the title of Sir, himself, — Samuel Appleton, the first emigrant to New England (in 1635), was of the seventh generation.

Following down the history of the family on American soil through five generations,* — all of them illus-

* See Memorial of Samuel Appleton, of Ipswich, Mass., with Genealogical Notices, &c., by Isaac Appleton Jewett. Boston: 1850.

trated by names associated with valuable services in Church or State, in peace or war, in some honorable profession or in some no less honorable department of useful industry, — during the larger part of the time at Ipswich, in Massachusetts, where the first emigrant settled, and more recently at New Ipswich, in New Hampshire, — we come to the subject of our memoir.

He was the seventh son of Isaac Appleton, whose habitual title of Deacon was doubtless a just recognition of the gravity of his character, and of the interest which he took in the religious institutions of the community in which he lived. The father of twelve children, ten of whom lived to maturity, Isaac may not have had the wealth, even if he had the will, to send all his boys to college. It may perhaps have damped his disposition for making scholars of the others, that his second son (Joseph) died so soon after taking his Bachelor's degree at Hanover. But the early education of his children was not neglected, either by him or by themselves. The school life and academy life of Nathan, certainly, seem to have been deeply impressed on his own memory. He was evidently an ambitious and a successful scholar. He pursued his studies until he was fitted to enter college; and, after a formal examination, he was regularly admitted to the freshman-class at Dartmouth College. The following passage from the "Sketches of Autobiography," which he committed to the writer of these pages, with his own hand, not long before his death, and which were drawn up about six years since, gives a vivid picture of his early days; and though it leaves the question unsettled, whether his stopping short at the very threshold of college life was owing to his father's preferences or his own, it shows conclusively that it was not from being turned by at the examination. Nathan was not of a complexion to be *turned by* from any thing which he undertook, either as boy or man; and Dartmouth lost a good scholar and a distinguished alumnus, when he declined the matriculation which she tendered to him, and to which his examination had fully entitled him.

"I was born at New Ipswich, according to the record, on the sixth day of October, 1779. The only tradition which I ever heard of my infancy is, that I was so near being carried off by a lung-fever, that preparations were making for laying me out. The earliest thing of which I have any recollection is the falling of the sash of a window, when I was in somebody's arms, upon the forefinger of my left hand, by which it was cruelly crushed, and the marks of which remain all my life. I have some recollection of going to school to the Widow Tillick, who taught me the letters by pointing them out with a fescue. I afterward attended the town-school, kept by a Mr. Hedge. I well recollect the trepidation with which I was seized, the first day of my attendance, at seeing a big boy, my cousin, called up, and receive a severe flogging. My first appearance in public was at this school at a very early age, when I recited 'Aurora, now fair daughter of the dawn,' to the great admiration of several old women, who particularly praised me in the lines, —

'I fix the chain to great Olympus' height,
And the vast world hangs trembling in my sight.'

I recollect that this was the first occasion of my appearing in jacket and trousers, and that they consisted of red calamanco. Mr. Hedge was unpopular with the older scholars: and, on occasion of some difficulty about the schoolhouse chimney, some of the bigger boys, being sent up into the garret to see what was the matter, took advantage of the opportunity to break down the chimney altogether; and thus was an end put to the school for the year. A new schoolhouse was built, about half way up the steep hill; which was then the only avenue through the middle of the town. At this I attended school several years during the winter, or as long as the town-school was kept. The only competition of the scholars was in spelling. . . . Rebecca Barrett (afterwards wife of Hon. Samuel Dana) and myself were generally at the head of the class; and there was more difficulty in making either of us change places, when at the head, than in running through all the rest of the class. My last master here was Mr. Dakin: and when I had got through the cube-root, and came to algebra, he frankly told me that he could go no farther with me; that I then knew as much as he did.

"About the year 1792, the Academy was established at New Ipswich. Mr. Hubbard was the preceptor, — a most worthy, excellent man. Under his tuition I was prepared for entering college. He gave exhibitions in very superior style. At one of them, I performed the part of Belcour in the 'West Indian;' at another, that of Marplot in the 'Busy-body.' In August, 1794, I made the journey to Hanover on horseback, in company with Charles Barrett and —— Bemis; where I was examined, and admitted to the freshman-class in Dartmouth College. It had, however, been decided, previously, that I should proceed no further in collegiate studies than the entry. My brother Samuel was in trade in New Ipswich, and had decided on trying his luck in Boston; and he proposed I should accompany him. Whether this proposal was thought more eligible than going to college by my father or myself, I cannot now say; but the result was, that it was determined that I should become a merchant, rather than a scholar."

In immediate sequence to the passage which has thus been quoted, is found the description of that first humble advent to Boston, which has already been sketched, but which is altogether too characteristic to be omitted in its proper connection and in his own words. It forms the preamble, too, of a brief account of the small beginnings of that mercantile career to which his energies were henceforth to be devoted, and which he was destined to pursue so successfully for himself, and with so much honor and advantage to the community in which he lived and died. His study of "book-keeping by double entry," and the emphatic testimony which he bears to its importance; his going to board with Mr. Sales for the benefit of speaking French; and his casual encounter of the late Mr. Justice Story in a small-pox hospital, where they first formed an acquaintance as fellow-patients, which ripened, in other years, into relations of the most cordial friendship and the highest mutual respect, — will not be unobserved by the reader. Mr. Appleton does not dilate on this latter incident; simply referring to certain "long discussions" which he heard there, and expressing himself "highly gratified." No doubt, the gratification was mutual. The one was always an excellent listener: the other was always an exuberant talker. If any thing could have relieved the tedium of that loathsome confinement, it must have been the ardent, hopeful, enthusiastic discourse of the youthful Story. How little could either of them have dreamed of the eminence they were to attain in after-life! Could they have inoculated each other at that moment with a little of their respective peculiarities, it would have been a gain, perhaps, to the social aptitudes of both.

"It was in October or November, 1794, that I took my departure for Boston. At that time, a stage ran from Boston to Groton. I was allowed a horse as far as Townsend, with my brother Eben to take him back. From there I footed it, with a pocket-handkerchief in my hand, which contained all my wearing apparel beside what was on my back. I arrived at Groton early in the afternoon; and, the next morning, took the stage for Boston. We dined at Concord; and I recollect, that, on passing Charlestown Bridge, the evening lamps were lighted. My brother commenced business in a small shop in Cornhill; to obtain which, he was obliged to purchase out the occupant, Mr. William P. White. His business consisted mostly in purchasing goods at auction, and selling them to country traders, for cash or short credit, for a small profit. He soon removed to a larger room, — No. 50, Cornhill. My first boarding-place was with a very old couple, — Mr. and Mrs. Ridgway, near Quaker Lane. I here became acquainted with Eliphalet Hale, whom I had known at New Ipswich Academy. He was from Jaffrey. He was in the service of John Cushing. From him I learned the first principles of book-keeping by double entry. With the assistance of Mair's Treatise, which I purchased, I soon opened a set of books for my brother; and, from that time, have never kept books in any other manner. I have always attributed a great portion of the failures which take place to a want of attention, or a want of knowledge, in the proper principles of book-keeping. In the year 1798, the yellow-fever prevailed in Boston. I was permitted to avail myself of the occasion to be inoculated for the small-pox at Dr. Aspinwall's hospital, at Brookline. Amongst the patients was Joseph Story, with whose acquaintance I was highly gratified. He was then a student at college. His long discussions with Dr. Aspinwall I well recollect. In 1799, my brother made his first voyage to Europe; leaving me in charge of his business, a part of which was to receive and dispose of his shipments of goods. After his return, we removed to a warehouse in State Street. I became of age in October, 1800. My brother proposed that I should become a partner with him, on terms which I considered liberal, and which I accepted. I had, at an early period, taken lessons in French. I afterward went to Mr. Sales', in Federal Court, as a boarder, in company with Henry Higginson, for the benefit of speaking French, which I continued a year or two."

Mr. Appleton had now entered on his majority; and opportunities were immediately at hand for enlarging his observation and experience, and for developing that spirit of sturdy self-reliance which was so leading an element of his character. He was sent out to England to purchase goods while Europe was in a state of war. The news of peace reached him on landing, and changed, of course, the whole condition and current of trade. He postpones his purchases, and travels on the Continent. Passing through the various cities of the Low Countries, he examines "with attention and interest the ruins of Valenciennes," whose long siege and bombardment, it seems, he had studied at the time they occurred, while he was a mere schoolboy. At Paris, he sees the treasures of art which Napoleon had accumulated as the spoils of his marvellous conquests in Italy; and, better still, he sees the great First Consul himself, at a grand military review, and at the exact period when his imperial ambition was just beginning to be distinctly foreshadowed.

He returns to America, and resumes his mercantile career; is happily married, and soon crosses the ocean again, for the health of his wife; meets the late Mr. Francis C. Lowell in Edinburgh, at the moment when he was first conceiving the policy to which the cotton manufacture of New England owes its origin, and holds an earnest and encouraging consultation with him in regard to it. Returning home again, he makes two visits to Washington in close succession, — the one a casual visit of curiosity, the other as a delegate from the merchants of Boston, — but both of them bringing him into familiar association with the men who controlled the affairs of the country, and thus preparing him to meet them afterwards as their peer and colleague; and all the while he is a merchant still, on the full tide of a prosperous and laborious business. But we must allow him to tell this part of his story, too, in his own brief and simple way; compressing, as he does, the incidents of more than ten years of his life into two or three manuscript pages.

"In November, 1801, I embarked for Liverpool for the purpose of purchasing goods in our regular business. On the pilot coming on board, we learned the news of peace, — the peace of Amiens. The first effect of this peace on American trade was very unfavorable. It caused many failures. Caution and curtailment were impressed upon me in all my letters from home. The day after the proclamation of the ratification of the peace, in April, 1802, I set off from London for the Continent, in company with A. W. Atherton. We embarked at Harwich for Helvoet Sluys, and visited the different cities of Holland and Belgium. I examined with attention and interest the ruins of Valenciennes, whose long siege and bombardment I had studied at the time in 1793. At Brussels we hired a cabriolet, which we finally kept all the way to Paris, where we arrived about the 1st of June. It was at the time of the Consulate; and Napoleon never stood higher in public estimation than then, as the restorer of peace and of the Catholic religion. At this time, however, his future ambition was shadowed forth, as the books were opened for subscription to answer the question, — *Bonaparte, sera-t-il Consul à vie?* Whilst in Paris, by buying an eligible seat, we had a very good opportunity to see Bonaparte at a grand review at the Place Carrousel. He was then thin and sallow. The museums and galleries of Paris then exhibited the treasures stolen from Italy and Belgium, and which were restored by the treaty of 1815. We returned to England in July; when the accounts from home came worse and worse, and I returned to Boston in September. I continued in business with my brother, with varied success, but, on the whole, with an average of prosperity, until 1809, when our copartnership was dissolved. My life had, thus far, been a laborious one. In 1806, I married Maria Theresa, the oldest daughter of Thomas Gold of Pittsfield. In 1810, I formed a copartnership with my brother Eben and Mr. Daniel P. Parker; which was brought to a close in 1813, in consequence of the war of 1812. The war, however, added very considerably to our profits. In 1810, I visited England on account of the health of my wife. In September, we made a tour into Scotland and the Lakes; passed the winter at Bath and Clifton; and in May, 1811, embarked for New York, where we arrived in June, with greatly restored health.

"Whilst in Edinburgh, I saw a good deal of Francis C. Lowell, Esq., who was there with his family. We had a good deal of conversation upon the subject of the cotton manufacture; and he told me that he had determined, before he returned, to make himself fully acquainted with the subject, with a view to the introduction of it at home. I urged him to do so, with an understanding that I should be ready to co-operate with him in such an undertaking. The war was declared in June, 1812. It so happened, that I was making a visit at Washington whilst it was in discussion in the Senate, in secret session; it having already passed the House. I was invited by Thomas R. Gold, my wife's uncle, a member from the State of New York, to join his mess, which was a large one; where I became acquainted with Harmanus Bleecker, and where Mr. Randolph, then in the opposition, was a frequent visitor. My time passed then very pleasantly. I dined at Mr. Foster's, the British minister's, on the Saturday preceding Wednesday, the 18th of June, when the War Bill finally passed the Senate. Mr. Foster had so little expectation of that result, that he actually purchased an ice-house on the day we dined with him, and on which the Senate passed a vote which made the final result certain. The general opinion amongst those opposed to the war was, that the Executive (Mr. Madison) was pushed up to make his war-message, but that he relied on the Senate to defeat it. The news of the death of Mr. Percival, and the impending repeal of the orders in council, reached Washington two days after the declaration of war. The orders in council were, in fact, repealed; and, in consequence, large shipments of goods were made for American account. To facilitate these shipments, under the alarming rumors of war which came from America, the British Government agreed to grant licenses or protections to American ships taking such goods, even should war between the two countries actually take place. On the arrival of these goods in the United States, they were taken possession of by the Government under the Non-intercourse Act, and bonds for the value required to be given before they could be delivered to the owners. The question of forfeiture was to be settled by Congress. As the amount involved was many millions of dollars, delegates were appointed from the different cities. Mr. John Gore and myself were appointed delegates from Boston. I accordingly proceeded to Washington at the commencement of the session, — December, 1812. Washington Irving (then engaged in trade) was one of the delegates from New York. We had hearings before the Committee of Ways and Means, of which Mr. Cheves was chairman. We were introduced to many of the distinguished members of Congress; as Mr. Clay (Speaker), Mr. Calhoun, Mr. Lowndes, &c. The Committee reported against us; Mr. Cheves, the chairman, dissenting. After a long debate, the House decided, by a close vote, in favor of cancelling the bonds.

"Whilst at Washington, and dressing one evening for the Naval Ball, an illumination was discovered to be lighting up in President's Square. It was soon known that the son of the Secretary of the Navy (Mr. Hamilton) had arrived in the city with the flag of the 'Macedonian,' captured by Decatur. This was afterward carried in triumph about the ballroom; which, of course, presented a scene of great excitement."

The next passage from the "Autobiographical Sketches," which we proceed with in its order, is a more considerable one; embracing an account of the first introduction of the power-loom into this country, and of the original establishment of the cotton manufacture at

Lowell. Much of it, if not the whole of it, has been given substantially, if not in the same words, in a pamphlet which Mr. Appleton published under his own name not many years ago. But the part which he took in so important an enterprise cannot be omitted in this connection; nor can it fairly be described in any language but his own. There is ground for thinking that he attached particular importance to its being reproduced in any memoir of which he might be the subject; and not without reason, — since it not merely unfolds the marvellous rise and progress of a great branch of American industry, but exhibits, so strikingly, the capacity of one who was largely concerned in the undertaking, to depict its various stages with simplicity, precision, and perfect candor. The testimony which he bears to the merits of others, and especially to the pre-eminent services of Mr. Lowell, is of no small historical value. It is the testimony not merely of a witness, but of an actor; and the seeming disclaimer of any particular credit for himself is altogether in keeping with his character, and furnishes a happy illustration of his unassuming disposition. Posterity will not fail to recognize him as one of the founders of that great manufacturing city, to which he boasts only to have given the name of his friend.

"In 1813, Mr. F. C. Lowell having returned from Europe, he and Mr. P. T. Jackson came to me one day on the Exchange, and stated that they had determined to establish a cotton manufactory, and that they had purchased a water-power in Waltham (Bemis's Paper-mills). They had obtained an act of incorporation; and Mr. Jackson had agreed to give up all other business, and take the management of the concern. The capital authorized by the charter was four hundred thousand dollars; but it was only intended to raise one hundred thousand dollars until the experiment was fairly tried. Of this sum, Mr. Lowell and Mr. Jackson, with his brothers, subscribed the greater part. They proposed to me to take ten thousand dollars of the stock. I told them, that, theoretically, I thought the business ought to succeed; but that all I had seen of its practical operation was unfavorable. I was therefore willing to take five thousand dollars of the stock, in order to see the experiment fairly tried, as I was sure it would be by Mr. Jackson, and would make no complaint if I lost the whole; but that I should decline taking a greater sum. They observed to me, that they wished to confine the stock in as few hands as possible; that they would offer the ten shares to one person, whom they named; and, if he declined taking them, I should have the five shares which I proposed. They soon afterward informed me, that the party they applied to made the same objection; and they therefore concluded to divide them between us. This was the origin of my connection with the cotton manufacture. On the organization of the company, I was appointed one of the directors; and, by constant communication with Messrs. Lowell and Jackson, was familiar with the progress of the concern.

"The first measure was to secure the services of Paul Moody, of Amesbury, whose skill as a mechanic was well known; and his success fully justified the choice. The power-loom was at this time being introduced in England; but its construction was kept very secret. Mr. Lowell had obtained all the information which was practicable about it, and was determined to perfect it himself. He was for months experimenting at a store in Broad Street, employing a man to turn a crank.

"It was not until the building was completed, and other machinery was running, that the first loom was ready for trial. Many little matters were to be overcome or adjusted before it would work perfectly. Mr. Lowell said to me, that he did not wish me to see it until it was complete, of which he would give me notice. At length, the time arrived; and he invited me to go out with him, and see the loom operate. I well recollect the state of satisfaction and admiration with which we sat by the hour watching the beautiful movement of this new and wonderful machine, destined, as it evidently was, to change the character of all textile industry. This was, I think, in the autumn of 1814. Mr. Lowell's loom was different in several particulars from the English loom, which was afterward made public. The introduction of the power-loom made several other changes necessary in the process of weaving. The first was in the dressing; for which Mr. Horrocks, of Stockport, obtained a patent, and of which Mr. Lowell obtained a drawing. On putting it in operation, an essential improvement was made upon it, by which its efficiency was more than doubled. This Waltham dressing-machine continues in use, with little change, from that time. The stop-motion of the machine for winding on the beams for dressing was original with this company. The greatest improvement was in the double speeder. The original fly-frame was made on no fixed principle for regulating the changing movements necessary in the process of filling a spool. Mr. Lowell undertook to make the numerous mathematical calculations necessary to perfect these complicated movements, which occupied him constantly for more than a week. Mr. Moody carried them into effect by constructing the machinery in conformity. Several trials at law were made under this patent; involving the nice question, whether a mathematical calculation could be the subject of a patent. The last great improvement consisted in a more slack spinning on throstle spindles; and the spinning of filling directly on the cops, without the process of winding.

"A pleasant anecdote is connected with this last invention. Mr. Shepherd, of Taunton, had a patent for a winding-machine, which was considered the best extant. Mr. Lowell was chaffering with him about purchasing the right of using them on a large scale, offering him some reduction from the price named. Mr. Shepherd refused; saying, 'You must have them: you know you cannot do without them; can you, Mr. Moody?' Mr. Moody replied, 'I am just thinking that I can spin the cops direct upon the bobbin.'—'You be hanged!' said Mr. S.: 'well, I accept your offer.'—'No,' said Mr. Lowell: 'it is too late.' From the first starting of the first power-loom, there was no hesitation or doubt about the success of this manufacture. The full capital of four hundred thousand dollars was soon filled up and expended; and an addition of two hundred thousand dollars was afterwards made by the purchase of the place below, in Watertown.

"After the peace in 1815, I formed a new copartnership with Mr. Benjamin C. Ward. I put in the capital, with the understanding that I was not to perform any of the labor of carrying on the business. I had acquired a fortune sufficient for my moderate desires; but I was unwilling to separate myself entirely from the operations of business. So far as the original object of this copartnership was concerned, — the importation of British goods, — it was unsuccessful, as I never recovered back my capital with simple interest; but an accidental circumstance occasioned its continuance until 1830. At the time the Waltham Company first began to produce cloth, there was but one place at which domestic goods were sold: this was at a shop in Cornhill, kept by Mr. Isaac Bowers, or rather by Mrs. Bowers. Accordingly, the first goods made were sent to Mrs. Bowers. As there was, at this time, only one loom in operation, the quantity accumulating was not very great. However, one day Mr. Lowell said to me, that there was one difficulty which he had not apprehended: the goods would not sell. We went together to see Mrs. Bowers. She said everybody praised the goods, and no objection was made to the price; but still they made no sales. I told Mr. Lowell, the next time they sent a parcel to town, to send them to the store of B. C. Ward and Co., and I would see what could be done.

"The article first made at Waltham was precisely the article of which a large portion of the cotton manufacture of the country has continued to consist, — a heavy sheeting of No. 14 yarn, thirty-seven inches wide, forty-four picks to the inch, and weighing something less than three yards to the pound. That it should have been so well suited to the public demand was matter of accident. At that time, it was supposed no quantity of cottons could be sold without being bleached; and the idea was to imitate the yard-wide goods of India. Mr. Lowell informed me that he would be satisfied with twenty-five cents the yard for the goods, although the nominal price was higher. I soon found a purchaser for the first parcel in Mr. Forsaith, an auctioneer; who sold them at auction at once, at something over thirty cents. We continued to sell them at auction for some time, with little variation of the price. This circumstance led to the company of B. C. Ward and Co. becoming permanently the selling agents. In the first instance, I found an interesting and agreeable occupation in paying attention to the sales; and made up the first account with a charge of one per cent commission, not as an adequate mercantile commission, but satisfactory under the circumstances. This rate of commission was continued, and finally became the established rate, under the great increase of the manufacture. Thus what was at the commencement rather unreasonably low, became, when the amount of sales concentrated in single houses amounted to millions of dollars, a desirable and profitable business.

"Under the influence of the war of 1812, the manufacture of cotton had greatly increased, especially in Rhode Island, but in a very imperfect manner. The effect of the peace of 1815 was ruinous to these manufacturers. In 1816, a new tariff was to be made. The Rhode-Island manufacturers were clamorous for a very high specific duty. Mr. Lowell was at Washington for a considerable time during the session of Congress. His views on the tariff were much more moderate; and he finally brought Mr. Lowndes and Mr. Calhoun to support the minimum of six and a quarter cents the square yard, which was carried. In June, 1816, Mr. Lowell having invited me to make a visit to Rhode Island with him in order to see the actual state of the manufacture, I was very happy to accept his proposition. At this time, the success of the power-loom at Waltham was no longer matter of speculation or opinion: it was a settled fact.

"We proceeded to Pawtucket. We called on Mr. Wilkinson, the maker of machinery. He took us into his establishment, — a large one. All was silent, — not a wheel in motion, not a man to be seen. He informed us that there was not a spindle running in Pawtucket: except a few in Slater's old mill, making yarns, all was dead and still. In reply to questions from Mr. Lowell, he stated, that, during the war, the profits of manufacturing were so great, that the inquiry was never made, whether any improvement could be made in machinery, but how soon it could be turned out. We saw several manufacturers: they were all sad and despairing. Mr. Lowell endeavored to assure them that the adoption of the power-loom would put a new face upon the manufacture; but they were incredulous: it might be so; but they were not disposed to believe it. We proceeded to Providence, and returned by the way of Taunton. We there stopped at the factory of Mr. Shepherd, who had put a power-loom in operation, acting vertically; that is to say, the web running up and down, and the lathe playing in the same way. It was evident that it could not succeed. By degrees, however, the manufacturers woke up to the fact, that the power-loom was an instrument which changed the whole character of the manufacture; and that, by adopting the other improvements which had been made in machinery, the tariff of 1816 was sufficiently protective. Mr. Lowell adopted an entire new arrangement, in order to save labor in passing from one process to another; and in so arranging all the machinery, that the entire product should be converted into cloth within the mill.

"It is remarkable how few changes, in this respect, have since been made from those established by him in the first mill built in Waltham. It is also remarkable how accurate were his calculations as to the expense at which goods could be made. He used to say, that the only circumstance which made him distrust his calculations was, that he could bring them to no other result but one which was too favorable to be credible. His calculations, however, did not lead him so far as to make him imagine that the same goods which were then selling at thirty cents a yard, would, at any time, be sold at six cents, and without a loss to the manufacturer, as has since been done. He died in 1817, beloved and respected by all who knew him. He is entitled to the credit of having introduced the new system in the cotton manufacture, under which it has grown up so rapidly; for, although Messrs. Jackson and Moody were men of unsurpassed energy and talent in their way, it was Mr. Lowell who was the informing soul, which gave direction and form to the whole proceeding.

"The success of the Waltham Company made me desirous of extending my interest in the same direction. I was of opinion, that the time had arrived when the manufacture and printing of calicoes might be successfully introduced in this country. In this opinion, Mr. Jackson coincided; and we set about discovering a water-power. At the suggestion of Mr. Charles H. Atherton of Amherst, N.H., we met him at a fall of the Souhegan River, about six miles from its entrance into the Merrimack; but the power was insufficient for our purpose. This was in the summer of 1821. In returning, we passed the Nashua River, without being aware of the existence of the fall which has since been made the source of so much power by the Nashua Company. We saw a small gristmill standing in the meadow near the road, with a dam of some six or seven feet. Soon after our return, I was at Waltham one day; when I was informed that Mr. Moody had lately been at Salisbury, where Mr. Worthen, his old partner, said to him, 'I hear, Messrs. Jackson and Appleton are looking out for water-power: why don't they buy up the Pawtucket Canal? that would give them the whole power of the Merrimack, with a fall of thirty feet.' On the strength of this, Mr. Moody had returned that way, and was satisfied with the extent of the power, and that Mr. Jackson was making inquiries on the subject. Mr. Jackson soon after called on me, and informed me that he had had a correspondence with Mr. Clark of Newburyport, the agent of the Pawtucket Company, and had ascertained that the stock of that company, and the lands necessary for using the water-power, could be purchased; and asked me what I thought of taking hold of it. He stated that his engagements at Waltham would not permit him to take the management of a new concern; but he mentioned Mr. Kirk Boott as having expressed a wish to take the management of an active manufacturing establishment, and that he had confidence in his possessing the proper talent for it.

After a discussion, it was agreed that he should consult Mr. Boott; and that, if he would join us, we would go on with it. He went at once to see Mr. Boott, and soon returned to inform me that Mr. Boott entered heartily into the project; and we set about making the purchases without delay. Until these were made, it was necessary to confine all knowledge of the project to our own three bosoms. Mr. Clark was employed to purchase the necessary lands, and such shares in the canal as were within his reach; whilst Mr. Henry Andrews was employed in purchasing up the shares owned in Boston. I recollect the first interview with Mr. Clark, at which he exhibited a rough sketch of the canal and adjoining lands, with the prices which he had ascertained they could be purchased for; and he was directed to go on and complete the purchases, taking the deeds in his own name, in order to prevent the project taking wind prematurely. The purchases were made accordingly for our equal joint account; each of us furnishing funds as required to Mr. Boott, who kept the accounts. Formal articles of association were then drawn up. They bear date Dec. 1, 1821; and are recorded in the records of the Merrimack Manufacturing Company, of which they form the germ. The six hundred shares were thus subscribed: —

Kirk Boott and J. W. Boott	180
N. Appleton	180
P. T. Jackson	180
Paul Moody	60
	600

"The Act of Incorporation of the Merrimack Manufacturing Company bears date 5th of February, 1822; recognizing the original association as the basis of the company. Our first visit to the spot was in the month of November, 1821, when a slight snow covered the ground. The party consisted of P. T. Jackson, Kirk Boott, Warren Dutton, Paul Moody, John W. Boott, and myself. We perambulated the grounds, and scanned the capabilities of the place; and the remark was made, that some of us might live to see the place contain twenty thousand inhabitants.

"On our first organization, we allowed Mr. Moody to be interested to the extent of ten per cent, or sixty out of six hundred shares. We soon after made an arrangement with the Waltham Company, making a mutual interest between the two companies. The canal was a work of great labor. The first water-wheel of the Merrimack Manufacturing Company was set in motion on the 1st of September, 1823. The business of printing calicoes was wholly new in this country. It is true, that, after it was known that this concern was going into operation for that purpose, two other companies were got up, — one at Dover, N.H.; the other at Taunton, — in both of which, goods were probably printed before they were by the Merrimack Company.

"The bringing the business of printing to any degree of perfection was a matter of difficulty and time. Mr. Allen Pollock thought himself competent to manage it, and was employed for some time. Through the good offices of Mr. Timothy Wiggin, Mr. Prince, of Manchester, was induced to come out, with his family; and has remained at the head of the establishment up to the present period (1855).

"The engraving of cylinders was a most important part of the process; and Mr. Boott made one voyage to England solely for the purpose of engaging engravers. It was then kept a very close mystery. Mr. Dana was employed as chemist. Through the superior skill and talent of Messrs. Boott, Prince, and Dana, the company was brought to the highest degree of success. In the mean time, Mr. Moody was transferred from Waltham to this place, having charge of the manufacture of machinery. Mr. Worthen had been employed at an early day. He was a man of superior mechanical genius, and his death was deeply regretted. The capital of the Merrimack Company was gradually increased, a division of the property betwixt that company and the Proprietors of the Locks and Canals was made, new companies were established, until this new creation became a city, by the name of Lowell. I may, perhaps, claim having given it the name. Several names had been suggested, but nothing fixed on. On meeting Mr. Boott one day, he said to me that the committee were ready to report the bill (in the Legislature). It only remained to fill the blank with the name. He said he considered it narrowed down to two, — Lowell or Derby. I said to him, 'Then Lowell, by all means;' and Lowell it was."

From the intimate acquaintance which Mr. Appleton had thus acquired with the history of the American cotton manufacture, and with all the details of its machinery and management from its earliest establishment in New England, he derived peculiar qualifications for the public services which he was soon called upon to render. No questions which have ever arisen in our country have given occasion to more important discussions, or more protracted and agitating controversies, than those which have related to our revenue system; and no feature of that system has been so frequently and so violently contested as that which looked to the encouragement of the manufacture of cotton on American soil. It has divided parties; it has arrayed State against State, and section against section; it has shaken the republic to its foundation. The mad design to rend the Union asunder forever, which has plunged us at last into so deplorable a conflict, owed not a little of its original impulse to the jealousies and antipathies which had arisen from a fancied antagonism between the interests of the cotton-growers of the South and the cotton-spinners of the North. It was in connection with the alleged injustice of a discriminating tariff, and during the very debate in which Mr. Appleton first took a prominent part in the Congress of the United States, that Mr. McDuffie originally promulgated the idea of "a glorious rebellion," by which South Carolina was to be freed from oppression. Few men were in the way of doing more to counteract this delusion, at this memorable period of its primary development, than Mr. Appleton; and no man improved his opportunities to better advantage. In the public journals, in commercial dictionaries or conversations-lexicons, in the Legislature of Massachusetts, in the Congress of the United States, his pen and his voice were always ready and always effective in demonstrating the fallacies of a doctrine, which would long ago have surrendered to Great Britain the undisputed monopoly of those textile fabrics by which the world was to be clothed, and for which the raw material was furnished, in so large a part, by the Southern States. If the forty-bale theory was at last demolished, it is hardly too much to say, that the weaver's beam which dealt the sturdiest blows, and did the largest share in the demolition, was wielded by the arm of Nathan Appleton.

He entered the Legislature of Massachusetts in 1815, and was re-elected one of the Boston representatives in 1816, 1821, 1823, 1824, and 1827. In 1830, he was chosen a member of the House of Representatives of the United States, after one of the most exciting and closely contested political struggles which Boston has ever witnessed. Declining a re-election in 1832, he was induced to resume the Boston seat in Congress, for a few months, in 1842. It so happened, that some of the most important discussions which have ever occurred on the subject of the tariff, in our National Legislature, were exactly coincident with his terms of service. Perhaps it would be more just to say, that he was selected for the candidacy, and induced to accept it, at these particular times, with a special view to his ability to grapple with the questions which were then plainly impending. Certain it is, he was there at the right moment, both for his own reputation, for the advantage of his constituents, and, still more, for the right understanding of those great problems of public policy with which his personal experience and practical sense had peculiarly fitted him to deal. But let us no longer detain our readers from his own plain and modest account of this part of his career, and of some of the services which he rendered to the cause of a discriminating revenue system.

"At the request of Dr. Lieber, I furnished him an article on the cotton manufacture, for his Dictionary. Mr. Condy Raguet, editor of the 'Banner of the Constitution,' in Philadelphia, ridiculed the idea therein expressed, that we could compete with Great Britain in the article of coarse cottons for exportation. This led to an anonymous correspondence, and the acceptance, on his part, of a proposition which I made him, to furnish him some articles on the cotton manufacture; which was accordingly done in six numbers, signed 'Statist,'—the last dated Aug. 31, 1831. In the first number, I stated that the fact of a constantly increasing export of these goods for a number of years, although then only amounting to a million of dollars, was proof of the fact, that we did furnish them in a fair competition with the British. The fact is adverted to, that we had introduced a manufacture which was a new article in commerce, containing a greater quantity of the raw material, with a less proportion of labor, than any thing then in use, and of course furnishing a cheaper and more economical article of general consumption. It was also contended, that we had, on the whole, a balance of advantages over England in this manufacture: which consisted, first, in the greater cheapness of water-power over steam, estimated as six hundred to three thousand eight hundred and forty; and, second, in the advantage of having the raw material nearer at hand, estimated at two cents the pound. (Cotton was then subject to a duty in England of five-eighths of a penny per pound.) Against these advantages, the only offset was a difference in the cost of machinery; which was estimated to cost fifty per cent more in the United States than in England.

"The second number took up the subject of labor, and gave documents to prove that the price then paid for labor in the cotton manufacture in England was as great or greater than was paid in the United States. This was owing to our employing females only, whilst the English employed a large proportion of men, especially as mule-spinners, earning very high wages; whilst we had improved throstle-spinning, operated wholly by females, so as to supersede, in a great measure, the use of mules. All this has been changed since by the introduction of self-acting mules.

"Mr. Raguet remarks, that 'the views presented in these two communications are calculated to make a stirring impression upon public opinion. To disprove the positions of our correspondent will require the aid of some of our mercantile friends.' He finally states his readiness to publish the opinions of 'Statist' upon the tariff, as well as information upon the finer branches of the cotton manufacture.

"In the third and fourth numbers, 'Statist' proceeds to describe the progress of cotton manufacture, which he finally divides into three classes: viz., first, the coarse goods which we were then exporting in considerable quantities; second, the finer descriptions of plain goods, as shirtings and sheetings, in which our own consumption was well supplied by our own manufacture; and, third, printed calicoes and other colored goods, of which we were then supposed to manufacture something more than one-half our consumption. The different bearing of the tariff on these classes is pointed out, — on the first, merely nominal; on the second, very trifling. 'It is in the higher branches of the third class only that the question of a reduction of duty pinches. Here the two contending tides of importation and manufacture meet: here is the sole action of the tariff.' In these and in No. 5, the question of the protective policy is discussed; and a good deal of stress is laid on the impolicy of subjecting our industry to the fluctuations taking place in other countries, of which the revulsion of 1829, in England, furnished a striking example.

"These speculations appear to have been rather distasteful to Mr. Raguet; for he declined to publish any thing further from the writer, unless he would avow his name, as he doubted the correctness of his statement of the cost of manufacturing coarse cottons. In my rejoinder, I gave him the abstract cost of the manufacture in an establishment, with a sample of the goods made, and a personal reference to a merchant in Philadelphia. He, in reply, says that a manufacturer to whom he showed the sample could not believe that such goods could be made for seven and one-third cents the pound, as I had stated; but, in consequence of what he considered concessions on my part, he invited me to a renewal of the correspondence. This I did not think proper to do; and so the correspondence ended. It will be seen that I took the same ground, in respect to coarse cottons, in the first speech which I made in Congress.

"About the year 1820, I was elected a member of the Massachusetts Legislature, for Boston, and at intervals for several years. At this time, party-spirit ran very low; and at last, under the administration of Mr. Monroe, may be fairly said to have died out. With a view to sustain John Quincy Adams for the Presidency, a final amalgamation of parties took place. I was present at the last caucus of the Federal members of the Legislature, at which the union was agreed to, which was consummated by the election of Levi Lincoln as Governor. I well recollect the first union caucus at the Exchange Coffee House, when it was amusing to see William Sullivan and Benjamin Russell harmonize with Major Melville and Ebenezer Clough. This harmony was somewhat disturbed by a new party, at first known as the Crawford party, afterward resolved into the all-powerful Jackson party. My first speech in public was in opposition to a specific tax on insurance-companies. I was for several years Chairman of the Committee of Finance, whose most important duty was the making of the tax-bill.

"In 1828, Mr. Calhoun, of Springfield, introduced a resolution approving the protective system, and moved a very early day for its consideration. I requested a later one; but, expecting I should oppose it, he declined. A friend, however, wishing to give me a chance to speak upon it, got a reconsideration carried. The speech which I made was any thing but an ultra one, and was very generally approved. In 1830, it was proposed to me to stand as candidate for Congress. I hesitated a good deal before I consented; which I did eventually, and was elected after a close contest. My competitor was Henry Lee, Esq.; and the election turned upon free trade or the protective principle. I took my seat in the Twenty-second Congress, December, 1831. Mr. Stevenson was chosen Speaker, and, in the appointment of the committees, placed me on that of Invalid Pensions. Considering that I was the representative of a greater commercial interest than any other individual in the House, and withal a practical merchant, this appointment could be considered in no other light than a spiteful revenge upon the city of Boston for having disappointed the administration in the choice of the representative. I took lodgings at Gadsby's, in company with Mr. Webster; each of us having one of the front parlors, in which we took our meals together every alternate week. At an early day in the session, Mr. Bouldin, of Virginia, introduced a resolution of inquiry as to the nature of the minimums recognized in our revenue-laws. A sort of desultory debate, during the morning hour, had gone on for several weeks; when it occurred to me as an occasion on which I might make a short speech. On mentioning it to Mr. Webster, he encouraged me to do so, and put me in the way cf getting the information which I wanted. The subject came up again on the 21st of January, when Mr. McDuffie made a most strenuous appeal against further debate on a mere question of inquiry; but, being prepared, I did not choose to let the opportunity go by. I undertook to show that South Carolina was the author of the system of minimums, which was only another name for specific duties, and a system capable of defence. It was introduced by Mr. Lowndes, as Chairman of the Committee of Ways and Means, in 1816. I took the occasion to state, that we could convert a pound of our cotton into the common cloth we were making for less money than the British could do. This being a fact well known to me, the statement was made advisedly, wishing the matter to stand on its true basis; but, being so contrary to the general impression, it quite alarmed some of the friends of the protective system, as I learned afterwards. My speech gave a new turn to the debate. It brought up McDuffie and Cambreling, and the debate occupied the whole day. The vote showed a majority of about twenty in favor of the protective system.

"The great business of that session was the framing a new tariff. The object was greatly to reduce the revenue, the debt being paid off, and, at the same time, to continue the principle of protecting American industry. There were several caucuses of the friends of protection. At one of them, Governor Davis and myself were appointed a committee to frame such a tariff. We accordingly framed one, making every thing free which did not interfere with our own productions. The subject was finally referred, in the House of Representatives, to the Committee on Manufactures, of which John Q. Adams was chairman. He applied to us for our project, which was substantially adopted in the tariff of 1832.

"The Committee of Ways and Means, of which Mr. McDuffie was chairman, made a report at an early period of the session, very elaborate and able; setting forth the theory, that all duties on imports were essentially and absolutely taxes upon the exports for which they were exchanged, better known as the forty-bale theory. As the argument was very plausible and specious, I determined to answer it, whenever the subject came up for discussion. With this view, I prepared an analysis of it with a good deal of care and time. When the subject of the tariff came up, Mr. McDuffie opened the discussion with an elaborate speech, especially addressed to me. He chose a place to deliver it directly by my side; and made it exceedingly personal, on the ground that we were rival manufacturers, — one operating with hoes and spades, the other with spindles and shuttles. As his speech contained nothing which was not set forth in his report, I determined to follow him at once with my answer; and, with this view, endeavored to get the floor. It was given to Mr. Crawford, of Pennsylvania; but, when he got through, the next morning, I obtained it. It was on the 30th of May, 1832. It so happened that Mr. McDuffie was not in the House during the first half of my speech. I regretted it; but there was no help for it. I determined from the first to treat his theory with great contempt, preserving all due respect to himself. He showed a good deal of spiteful ill nature in a subsequent speech. I drew up a copy of my speech, which was printed by Gales and Seaton. Mr. McDuffie's was in the hands of Duff Greene. On inquiring of the latter the cause of the long delay in the appearance of the speech, he informed me that Mr. McDuffie found it hard to please himself; that, after setting it up, he had to take it down, and make an entire new copy. After this, I thought it proper to keep mine back till his had appeared. His speech, as printed, is much less personal to myself than as it was delivered. I received a good many compliments on this speech. Mr. McDuffie had always maintained, that, whilst his theory was much abused in the general, no one had undertaken to show the fallacy of his position. This was what I endeavored to do; with what success, it was for others to judge. A very elaborate review of it was published in the 'National Intelligencer,' altogether favorable. I never knew the writer. Since Mr. Webster's death, I have found amongst my papers the following very flattering note from him after reading this speech: —

Mr. Webster to N. Appleton, after reading his Speech, June, 1832.

DEAR SIR, — It appears to me you have completely refuted each and every of Mr. McDuffie's propositions. I see no vestige left of one of his arguments. You will see I have made a remark or two on the tenth, the fourteenth, and seventeenth pages. The speech is a model of close reasoning on an abstruse subject.

Yours truly, D. WEBSTER.

MR. APPLETON.

"I have long since been of opinion that this South-Carolina theory was only pretence. It was thought a convenient cover to what has continued their favorite idea, — the separation of the Slave States from the rest of the Union.

"The renewal of the charter of the Bank of the United States was one of the exciting topics of this session of Congress. The first question was on the reference of the subject, as mentioned in the President's Message. The friends of the bank proposed referring it to the Committee of Ways and Means; those opposed to it, to a Special Committee. I was desirous to introduce several amendments, and was in favor of the Special Committee; but it soon became apparent that the whole struggle was, bank or no bank. No one seemed to trouble himself much about its character. Its friends took every thing from Mr. Biddle. His *ipse dixit* was law and gospel with them. My faith in Mr. Biddle had at that time been materially shaken; and I accordingly laid on the table, and had printed, some amendments, which I intended at the proper time to offer to the bill. But the bill which had passed the Senate was delayed to the latest moment of the session, in consequence of a Committee of Examination having been sent to Philadelphia. The cholera had broken out in New York. It was believed, that if the bill was referred to the Committee of the Whole, and subjected to amendment, it would be lost. It was therefore decided by its friends to avoid going into committee, but to pass the bill exactly as it came from the Senate. I was therefore obliged to abandon my design, or put myself in a hopeless opposition to all my friends; which I did not choose to do. Mr. Clay made a forcible appeal to me, considering that the fate of the Whig cause depended on passing the measure. He said, with an oath, 'Should Jackson veto it, I will veto him!' He was mistaken: Jackson did veto it, but was not himself vetoed. On my return from Congress, I found New York a deserted city, on account of the cholera. On coming into Broadway from the Battery, all was silent as death; not a person to be seen. On reaching Bunker's Hotel, the only person visible was a member of Congress from Connecticut; like myself, on his way home.

"On my return to Congress, at the second session (December, 1832), South Carolina was in a state of semi-rebellion. General Jackson, by his admirable proclamation (written by Mr. Livingston), had dealt her a sort of death-blow.

"At the same time, in his message and in the report of the Secretary of the Treasury, the ground was taken, that the tariff must be reduced. The reason assigned was, that it would produce too much revenue; the ground assumed being, that, at the former session, Congress had not carried out the recommendation of the Executive in this particular. It is true, the House had called on Mr. McLane, the Secretary of the Treasury, for his project of a bill; which he furnished, and which was adopted with certain modifications and alterations. I was under the impression, that the reductions which we had made in his bill were as great, or greater than our additions. I was therefore much gratified, in making an examination into this matter, to find, that, so far from the statement of the Executive being true, we had actually made reductions in the duties, on the basis assumed (the import of 1831), of a million of dollars beyond those presented in the bill of Mr. McLane, the Secretary of the Treasury. The Committee of Ways and Means reported a bill to reduce the duties, in conformity with the Presidential recommendation (called Verplanck's Bill). On this bill I felt it my duty to make a speech; which I accordingly did on the 23d of January, 1833, in which I dwelt pretty decidedly on the fact, that the assertion of the President, that we had not carried out the views of the Secretary in respect to the reduction of the revenue, was not correct, with the proof of it exhibited in figures. I afterward introduced a resolution, calling on the Secretary to show how he came to the result which he had stated. His answer did not come in till near the close of the session, and was not printed until all the measures were completed. He was, however, compelled to admit, that our bill reduced the duties more than the one he sent us. All this was accompanied with a very wry face, and the attempt to bring in new elements of calculation.

"In the course of my speech, I took the bold measure of introducing an exhibition of the cotton manufacture, which I had reason to believe had a very good effect. In the mean time, Mr. Clay had brought forward his Compromise Bill; reducing the duties gradually until 1842. On his arrival at Washington, he had consulted Governor Davis and myself, urging our co-operation in the measure; but, as we viewed it an abandonment of the principle of protection, we refused to do so. He brought it forward, nevertheless. Verplank's Bill labored very hard: and the administration, at length despairing of carrying it, decided in caucus to adopt Mr. Clay's Compromise Bill; which was accordingly introduced, and carried through both Houses, almost without debate.

"My wife was suffering from a complaint of the lungs. Dr. Warren was of opinion that she would doubtless hold out during the winter, and promised to advise me in time of any alarming change. Early in February, I received such a letter, and returned to Boston in great haste, but, alas! too late. She died on the 10th, — the day before my arrival. I returned to Washington, at the urgent request of some of my friends, a short time before the close of the session.

"In 1842, Robert C. Winthrop was the member of the House of Representatives from the District of Suffolk. In May, he resigned his seat in consequence of the illness and impending death of his wife. A successor must be appointed on the instant. The public looked to either Abbott Lawrence or myself to fill the vacancy. Mr. Lawrence was appointed commissioner, on the part of Massachusetts, to settle the Maine boundary question with Lord Ashburton: so that I found myself under an almost unavoidable necessity of consenting to take the place; which I did very reluctantly, and took my seat in the Twenty-seventh Congress on the 9th of June. The tariff was again the chief subject of interest. Mr. Clay's compromise had run out on the 1st of July; and it was a question, whether any duties whatever could be legally collected. Matters were in a very complicated state, in consequence of the quarrel between President Tyler and his own party, the Whigs. Again I felt bound to make a speech on the tariff; so that, in the three sessions in which I was a member of Congress, I was called on to make three speeches on the tariff, on three different bills. Finally, with extreme difficulty, the tariff of 1842 was carried. After the close of the session, I resigned my seat in Congress, in conformity with my own wishes, and also to make room for the return of Mr. Winthrop, the death of whose wife had taken place in the mean time. During my residence at Washington, I took the place of Mr. Winthrop at Mr. Birth's, with Messrs. Granger, Kennedy, and Saltonstall, — a most agreeable party. Mr. Fillmore was chairman of the Committee of Ways and Means; and, as I was invited to be present at several of their meetings, I became quite intimate with him. The manner in which he discharged the office of chairman of the Committee of Ways and Means showed great resources and much tact. He won my entire esteem and respect."

But the subject of the tariff is by no means the only one on which Mr. Appleton has written and spoken with unsurpassed ability. His attention was early called to the banking system of Massachusetts, and to the currency of the United States; and he kept an intelligent and vigilant eye upon them both, to the end of his life. He was ever ready with suggestions, as prudent as they were prompt, for remedying the embarrassments or averting the disasters to which a paper circulation is so peculiarly liable; and few men have done more than he has done towards sustaining public credit, and reviving public confidence, in those seasons of pressure and panic by which the speculating spirit of our country has been so often overtaken. Rarely, indeed, has such a season occurred, without calling forth from him a letter, a newspaper article or series of articles, a speech or an essay, which has given the lead and direction to public sentiment, far beyond the limits of the community to which it was immediately addressed. He had a peculiar faculty of disentangling the intricacies of a financial or commercial question, and of presenting it in a form intelligible to the common mind. In this respect, among the men of the last half-century, he was only second, if second at all, to the late Mr. Albert Gallatin, with many of whose views he sympathized, and with whom he shared the enviable distinction of having recalled the commercial and banking community to a sense of what was just and honest, in many an hour when they were tempted to seek relief from embarrassment by the postponement of acknowledged obligations. The key to his whole policy, on questions of finance and currency, was the stern integrity of his own character; and he demanded, of those who managed the banking institutions of the land, only the same strictness in the fulfilment of engagements which he ever exhibited in his own individual transactions. His principal essay on the currency, as published in 1841, and republished with additions in 1857, is almost worthy of being studied in the schools, as an elementary manual on this seemingly difficult subject, which it simplifies to the level of the most ordinary comprehension. There are those among us who well remember the attention it excited at Washington, among public men from the South as well as the North, when it was first received there, at a moment of great financial perplexity; and the astonishment which was expressed, that a little plain, practical, unpretending common sense and common honesty had dispelled so many of the seeming mysteries of currency and exchange.

We have seen, in our last citation, that Mr. Appleton early distrusted the policy and principles of the late Mr. Biddle, and had some pretty independent views in regard to Mr. Biddle's Bank. We shall see more of this in the account of his relations to this question of banks and currency, as given in the extracts from his Autobiography, with which we now proceed: —

"The establishment of country banks in Massachusetts commenced about the year 1800. As their bills found a general circulation, the business was profitable, and the increase of country banks was rapid. As the bills accumulated in Boston, something must be done with them. At one time, the Boston banks received them; but the sending them home for payment was very unpopular. A nondescript association, called the Boston Exchange Office, was chartered, with a capital consisting of 'current bank-bills,' and authorized to receive deposits and make discounts in that currency: but the brokers would send home the bills of the most accessible banks, and the discount on country-bank notes; or, in the language of the day, the premium on Boston money continued to increase. A lawyer of Boston, named Andrew Dexter, undertook a tremendous speculation, — no less than the control of the circulating medium of New England. He obtained the control of the Boston Exchange Office; of a number of distant country banks; of the Berkshire, at Pittsfield; the Bangor, at Bangor; and especially the Farmers' Exchange, in Rhode Island. But, by an act of consummate folly, he invested the funds they placed within his control in an enormous building, known by the name of the Boston Exchange. He and all the country banks became pressed for means. The banks threw every obstacle in the way of payment of their bills, giving drafts on their agents at longer and longer time, until it reached three months, and the discount increased until it reached five per cent. At the same time, these bills continued to be received in payment in the country trade at par. Under these circumstances, there was a general disposition to resist so great an abuse. I undertook to form a plan for putting an end to it. At this time (1808), there was no penalty on the banks of Massachusetts for delay of payment, except simple interest and the costs of suit. The only power of coercion consisted in multiplying suits. I obtained a subscription of a hundred dollars each, from one hundred individuals and firms; which fund was placed in the hands of William Cochran, a broker, for management. We addressed a circular, which I drew up, addressed to all the country banks, informing them of our determination to put an end to the system of evasion and delay by legal means. The first call was on the Northampton Bank, which had lately gone into new hands; who were putting out their bills freely, with a view of playing the non-payment game. They began paying in fourpence-halfpennies. The agent employed, Lewis Tappan, was instructed to go on counting the money tendered him, but to inform the cashier, that, if they turned him out of the bank till he was ready to go, he should bring separate suits in behalf of all the parties interested in the several demands which he made; and so on, from day to day. After holding out until a late hour, the bank finally gave in, and gave a draft at a few days' sight on the agent in Boston. No other bank thought proper to attempt resistance. Dexter's banks all fell into discredit, and ceased to have any currency.

"A system of most barefaced fraud was discovered in connection with the Farmers' Exchange Bank, which compelled Mr. Dexter to leave the State. A most violent paralysis and crisis followed in reference to the circulation of country-bank notes. Nearly all the country banks, having considerable circulation, stopped payment; but those which were really solvent soon acquired the means of resumption. Some finally liquidated in full; but a great number never paid any thing. The result of this lesson was a correction of public opinion in relation to bank circulation. The general sympathy for country banks ceased: they were left to stand on their own merits. During this period, there was a good deal of discussion in the newspapers, in which I took a part.

"In the course of the war with England in 1814, the banks

of New York stopped payment, or, in the language of the day, *suspended* payment in specie; and all the South and West followed suit. At this time, the banks in Boston were very rich in specie. Neither the banks nor the citizens had gone into the war loans, as both had done in New York and Philadelphia; nor had her merchants taken much part in the wild speculations in merchandise which prevailed in other parts of the country. The question arose, whether the Boston banks should or could continue to pay specie whilst all the rest of the country had suspended. Public opinion was a good deal divided.

"Some very intelligent men took the ground, that it was absurd for Boston to think of paying specie whilst the banks of all the rest of the country had suspended. I was a director of the Boston Bank, and took ground with those who held that it was a mistake and a disgrace to suspend, except under a dire necessity; that not only did no such necessity exist, but the fact that all the other banks of the country were in a state of suspense made it easier for those of Boston to continue to pay specie; inasmuch as specie, like every thing else, was sure to flow where it was in use, or wanted, rather than to places where it had ceased to have any occupation. The event justified these views. Boston maintained her integrity in her currency, not only during the war, but during the long period of Southern suspension after the peace. The discount on the currency of Philadelphia reached twenty per cent. Boston felt no pressure on her money-market until the preparations for resumption after the establishment of the United-States Bank. She escaped, in a great measure, the terrible revulsion ever resulting from the restoration of a sound currency, after the existence, for a long period, of a depreciated one. This was fully developed in 1819. Boston suffered from her connection with New York and the South, but scarcely at all from her operations at home. During this period of suspension, I wrote frequently in the newspapers, especially a series of three or four numbers in the daily 'Advertiser,' under the head, 'Will the Southern Banks again pay Specie?' also a review of the Report of the Secretary of the Treasury (Mr. Dallas), severely censuring his action after the peace. I also wrote a review of Mr. Crawford's Report in 1820, in which he made several mistakes in relation to the currency of New England during the period of Southern suspension.

"In 1834, the country was deeply excited by the warfare carried on by General Jackson against the United-States Bank. At a public meeting in Boston, a committee was appointed to proceed to Washington with a memorial to Congress on the subject, of which I was appointed chairman. Nothing could have surprised me more than this appointment, as it was well known that I was of opinion that Mr. Biddle had already carried the system of contraction farther than was necessary. I was, therefore, disposed to decline the appointment. I learned, however, that I had been nominated for this office because of this opinion; and I finally concluded to accept it. On arriving in New York, I, with some others of the committee, called upon James G. King and Mr. Gallatin, who were members of a New-York Committee. We found the dissatisfaction with Mr. Biddle very ripe, and that they had given him an ultimatum, which he must accept, or be denounced at the adjourned public meeting as unnecessarily pressing upon the mercantile community. Mr. Gallatin read to us a report which he had prepared to meet the contingency. The meeting was to be held the next day. In the evening, who should appear at Bunker's, where the committee stopped, but Mr. Biddle himself! In the course of the evening, Mr. P. T. Jackson, Mr. Henry Lee, and myself, invited him to a private conference, at which we told him some home truths, — that our community ought not and would not sustain him in further pressure, which he very well knew was not necessary for the safety of the bank, and in which his whole object was to coerce a charter through the distresses of the mercantile community. He listened to us; but we could get very little from him but the merest commonplace. Soon after our arrival at Washington, I received, as I had previously arranged, a letter from Mr. King, saying that Mr. Biddle had yielded to the requisitions of the New-York Committee. Of course, the pressure of the money-market would, in a great measure, cease.

This intelligence was not altogether agreeable to all my political friends, so entirely does a political object override all other considerations. The arrangement with the New-York banks was only for a month; at the end of which, Mr. Biddle was reckless enough to put an end to it, and renew the pressure with even greater violence than before. But Congress adjourned soon after; when he gave up the chase, changed his tune, and increased the discounts of the bank some ten millions in the course of six months: —

1st September, 1834	$47,059,000
1st June, 1835	63,649,000

"In 1831, I published a pamphlet, with the title 'An Examination of the Banking System of Massachusetts, in Reference to the Renewal of the Bank Charters.' This was published without my name; but, as I freely avowed the authorship, it was generally understood. As it objected to granting the right of circulation to banks with capitals of less than five hundred thousand dollars, it was opposed by the country-bank interest, and called forth several pamphlets in answer. It took the ground, that the tax should apply wholly and only to the right of circulation. 'The tax can only be justified as the grant of a privilege under a right especially belonging to the State, that of regulating the currency;' not the legal currency transferred to the United States, but of bank-notes, which may be considered a conventional currency, depending wholly on the choice or pleasure of the receiver. My object in publishing this pamphlet was to put forward certain leading principles which I deemed correct, rather than any expectation of producing an actual change in the legislation of Massachusetts at that time.

"In 1835–6, a very remarkable state of over-trade existed; the immediate cause of it being an arrangement by which certain London houses allowed themselves to be drawn upon by houses in America, without funds in hand, but with an understanding, that, before the maturity of the bills so drawn, other bills, by other parties, should be substituted for those falling due.

"Whilst these bills could be discounted by the Bank of England, all went smoothly; and the system went on until the amount of the accommodation-bills, drawn upon nothing, became excessive. The Bank of England became alarmed at the amount, and refused to discount them.

"The failure of several large houses took place; others could only be saved by large remittances from America. This demand produced a call on the banks for specie; a violent pressure upon the money-market took place; a number of failures wholly unprecedented occurred in New York; the panic was tremendous; and at length, after a struggle of a month, the banks of New York yielded to the storm, and suspended specie payments, about the 1st of April, 1837. The banks throughout the whole country followed suit with great joy and alacrity. I was in Europe at the time, but returned in September, 1837. The banks of New York had got from the Legislature an extension of this suspension for a year; which expired in May, 1838. A call was made for a convention to meet in New York in April, to consider the subject of a general resumption. In November, 1837, I commenced a series of four numbers in the 'Boston Daily Advertiser,' advocating an early resumption of specie payments, and the sending delegates to the proposed convention at New York. The idea of resumption caused great alarm, and met with much opposition; but it was agreed to send delegates to the convention. I was, however, carefully excluded, as too radical in favor of resumption. Philadelphia, under the influence of Mr. Biddle, was utterly opposed to resumption, and persuaded Boston to go with her. Under the influence of Mr. Gallatin and Mr. Ward (of Prime, Ward, and King), the Legislature of New York was prevented granting a further extension; and the banks of New York actually resumed about the 1st of May. To assist the resumption, at the suggestion of James G. King, then in England, the Bank of England sent out by him a million of sovereigns, to be remitted for in bills of exchange then below par; under the influence of which, both Boston and Philadelphia resumed soon after.

"I was in Philadelphia about this time, and had a conversation with Mr. Biddle, in the course of which I was exceedingly disgusted with the views which he expressed. There can be but little doubt that he contemplated compelling the New-York banks again to suspend, and was in fact defeated by this timely supply of gold from the Bank of England.

"In 1840, Mr. Clay determined to bring forward his project for another Bank of the United States. I published, with my name, a pamphlet on 'Currency and Banking,' one motive of which was to show the danger from an institution of so great power. I had become satisfied, from my own observation, that it was a power too great to be intrusted to any one man.

"In 1839 (October), the Bank of the United States, acting under its Pennsylvania charter, again suspended payment, and proved desperately insolvent; carrying with it the Philadelphia banks, who foolishly involved themselves in its fortunes, from which they were only relieved by a large loan from Boston and New York. In arranging this loan, I took a leading and active part. Philadelphia did resume in consequence, on the 15th of January, 1841; but the Bank of the United States broke down after ten days' trial. The other banks of Philadelphia again followed suit, and did not finally resume until ——.

"During all this period, from 1837, I was frequently writing for the newspapers in Boston and Philadelphia, urging upon Philadelphia and the South to restore their currency."

The few remaining pages of the "Sketches of Autobiography" are almost wholly taken up with the account of another and more extensive tour in Europe, and with the domestic incidents by which it was occasioned and attended. There is nothing of particular interest or value in it, except inasmuch as it is eminently characteristic of the writer. It gives facts and names and dates, without the slightest attempt to describe the wonders of nature or of art which came within his view, or to express the emotions which they were calculated to excite. It was enough, for his own satisfaction, to say that he saw such places and persons and things. He had never studied the style of a word-painter; and the impressions which he received were probably rather practical than poetical. On his arrival at Geneva, he says only, "From thence made an excursion to Chamouni, and back to Geneva: was much interested in this excursion." Mont Blanc was certainly never dismissed with a simpler or less rapturous allusion. We have no idea that the grandeur of the Alps was lost upon him, or that he failed to appreciate the sublimity of the scenes which he had witnessed; but we may presently have reason for thinking, that the peculiar interest of the excursion was derived from his finding marks upon the rocks in that region, which concurred with some observations previously made by him at home.

More gratifying to him, however, we doubt not, than this view of "the monarch of mountains," or even than the presentation to the monarch of France, and the ball at the Tuileries, which he afterwards mentions, was the visit with which he concludes the account, as if it were the very climax of the whole tour, — the visit to the county of Suffolk, to the parishes of Great and Little Waldingfield, and to Holbrooke Hall, where his progenitors had resided in years long past. As he entered that old manor-house, and surveyed the ancestral seat, and then looked on the "beautiful genealogy" which his good friend Mr. Almack had so kindly prepared for him, he may well have experienced some emotions of pride, that the family tree had suffered nothing by transplantation; that "leaves and stalks, *vert*," had proved to be something more than a mere token of heraldry; and that the name of Appleton was (to say the least) as worthily distinguished at that moment, in his own person and in those immediately connected with him, as it had been during any of the six or seven generations in which it had either worn a title of knighthood, or been associated with the gentry of England. That old Suffolk soil must have contained its full share of English grit; and the stock which came from it has, in this instance certainly, proved hardy and rugged enough to repel all ideas of American degeneracy. But the "Sketches" must once more speak for themselves: —

"I declined being a candidate for re-election to the Twenty-third Congress, because political life was not much to my taste, but particularly as inconsistent to my duty to my family as it was then situated. In 1835 my son Charles made a tour to the South, on account of his health; but returned in a worse state than he left, and, in the course of the summer, fell a victim to his disease. One of my daughters was in delicate health, and I was advised by Dr. Warren to take a voyage to Europe. Accordingly, in November, with my son Thomas and two daughters, I embarked at New York for Havre, where we arrived about the middle of December, the thermometer about zero, which continued till we reached Paris. I was very happy to meet at Havre my old friend J. B. Greene, whom I had not seen for many years, and who gave us a most cordial reception. After a few weeks at Paris, we proceeded to Italy by way of Lyons, Marseilles, and the Corniche, or maritime Alp road. At Marseilles we passed two or three days; dined with the brothers Rabout, who lived with their interesting mother, whose husband and their father had fallen a sacrifice to the revolution. We also became acquainted with Mrs. Fitch, and Mr. Oxnard's interesting family. We spent a day at Toulon, and at Genoa dined with Mr. Campbell, the American Consul, who informed me that a gentleman was in the city with a commission for the same office, but who, after consulting him, concluded to keep it in his pocket. We admired the old palaces, full of old pictures, and the quaint old narrow streets, in which was barely room for a jackass with panniers to pass. By Carrara and Pisa and Florence, we went to Sienna, where we visited the famous gallery of old pictures, and other curiosities of old times. At Rome we passed many weeks; visited all the galleries, churches, &c., Tivoli and Tusculum. We remained through the ceremonies of Holy Week, which should close with the illumination of St. Peter's and the Girandola from the Castle of St. Angelo; but, owing to bad weather, these were postponed from day to day for a week, when the idea was abandoned. We then set out for Naples, where we passed our time most agreeably, visiting Pompeii, Vesuvius, Pæstum, Baiæ, &c. The ruins of Pompeii and the Museum are the most interesting objects to be found anywhere. Here we met Mr. and Mrs. Sidney Brooks; and from Naples we took steamboat for Leghorn, where we spent two or three days, and enjoyed some musical parties at Mr. Grant's. Hence to Bologna, Modena, Parma, Mantua, Verona. The alarming accounts of the cholera prevented our going to Venice, to our great regret; but we proceeded to Milan and Como, where we made an excursion up the Lake, then to Lake Maggiore and the Simplon to Brigg, and down the Rhone to Geneva. From thence we made an excursion to Chamouni, and back to Geneva: I was much interested in this excursion. We proceeded down the Lake to Lausanne; thence to Neufchâtel, Morat, Berne by Thun, to Interlachen; and made an excursion over the Col—— to the Faulhorn, where we slept at the temporary house, the highest sleeping-place in Europe; thence by Brientz to Interlachen; and thence to Berne, Lucerne, and Zürich. One of our party was William Appleton, son of William Appleton; a sweet youth, who, for some time, had been suffering from a disease of the lungs. We reached Schaffhausen, when he was unable to proceed further. We were at the hotel, where he had every attention. He lingered on for some weeks, when, after giving particular directions for the disposition of his collections, he peacefully and sweetly closed his eyes at the age of twenty.

"It so happened that the Rev. J. M. (afterward Bishop) Wainwright arrived at the hotel the day after his death, and consented to stay, and perform the funeral service. The keeper of the hotel informed me, that several gentlemen of the place were desirous of attending the funeral; to which, of course, I assented. There was quite a procession to the burying-ground, where I obtained a lot in perpetuity, and afterward sent a monumental stone from Paris.

"We afterward proceeded to Friburg, Strasburg, Baden-Baden, Heidelburg, Darmstadt, Frankfort, to Mayence. Here both my daughters were attacked with what the physician called a 'gastric fever,' by which we were detained six weeks. During this period, Thomas and myself made excursions to the chateau of Prince Metternich, at Johannisburg, and to Wisbaden. On the 2d November, with snow on the ground, we left Mayence for Paris, *viâ* Metz, Chalons, Rheims, Meaux, where we found apartments engaged for us at Meurice's. We left them, however, for very handsome apartments, Rue de Rivoli 10 *bis*, which I took for the winter. They were the property of a French officer, who married the widow of a rich Marseilles merchant; but who, belonging to the other party, was out of place under Louis Philippe.

"During the winter, we attended the various public amusements of Paris, saw all the sights, attended the weekly soirées of General Cass, were presented at court, and accepted invitations to the grand ball at the Tuileries, — a very splendid affair. We frequently attended Mr. Walsh's soirées, where were collected many of the savans.

"About April 20, we left Paris for Brussels. There had been a heavy snow-storm, and we met with many drifts on the sides of the road. We passed two or three days at Brussels, visited Waterloo, but were prevented reaching Hougomont by the road being blocked up with snow. Proceeding to Rotterdam, Amsterdam, and the Hague, we took the steamer at Rotterdam for London, where we arrived on the 2d May: the passage up the Thames was very interesting. We took rooms at the Brunswick Hotel, Jermyn Street; attended Epsom races, the Opera, &c.; made an excursion to Waldingfield; called on the rector of Great Waldingfield, who handed me the beautiful genealogy of the Appletons, drawn by Mr. Almack, now in my possession; visited both churches and Holbrooke Hall with much interest."

We come, at last, to the passage which forms the abrupt conclusion of these fragmentary sketches, and which at once betrays the source of that peculiar gratification which Mr. Appleton derived from his Alpine tour, and exhibits him in connection with subjects of investigation quite apart from those in which we have hitherto found him engaged: —

"My attention was early called to the subject of geology, to which I was attracted by the articles in the different reviews. I had been accidentally led to notice the striated surface of rocks, where they had not been acted upon by the atmosphere. For several years, I carried with me, in travelling, a pocket compass, and made my observations wherever I had opportunity. I ascertained that the same state of the rock surfaces existed from Canada to the District of Columbia, with grooves all running in the same direction. I was greatly surprised that this fact had never been noticed by geologists, which induced me to write an article to call their attention to it. I offered it to a work then published at Cambridge, edited by Dr. Webster and Mr. Treadwell: they objected to publish it, as indulging too much in theory, unless I would affix my name to it, to which they urged me. To this I would not consent, and sent it to Mr. Silliman, who published it in his journal of October, 1826. I only considered it important for its facts, which have since been the subject of great interest, and given rise to much discussion.

"It so happened, that in driving one day with Captain Basil Hall, and stopping to examine a geological formation, in the course of conversation, he asked me if I was the author of an article in Silliman's Journal on this subject. On my answering that I was, he stated to me, that his attention to it had been called by his father, Sir James Hall, who had published an article in the Edinburgh Philosophical Transactions, describing very nearly the same state of things, on one of the mountains of Scotland. This was the first intimation which I had, that these important phenomena had been observed anywhere at that time. The subject has been since very fully gone into by Dr. Jackson, in his Geology of Maine; and Professor Hitchcock, in that of Massachusetts. The theories of glaciers and icebergs have been introduced to account for their striæ with the accompanying alluvium, but with little satisfaction to a careful observer, as I think.

"When in Switzerland, I noticed there some marks on the rocks near the tops of some of the mountains, as on the Col de Forclaz, near the glacier de Rosenlaui and on the entrance into Chamouni, in situations directly the reverse of the ravines, into which alone glaciers can act."

Mr. Appleton had evidently cultivated those habits of close observation and careful discrimination which belong to the successful pursuit of natural science; and, for one who studied it only as an amateur, had become no mean proficient in geology. The superficial scratches which he had observed on the rocks, and to which he had so early called the attention of others, have given rise to a theory, which has since been much contested among scientific men. But he had decided opinions on this, as he had on almost all other questions which he undertook to examine at all; and he had a decided manner of expressing those opinions. He did not seek controversy, perhaps; but he rather relished it, and certainly never shrunk from it. Nor did he ever fail to conduct it with ability, good temper, and unyielding persistency. He seemed always ready, and always able, to give a reason for the faith that was in him, whether that faith related to matters commercial or political, to questions of morals or of science, to things temporal or to things eternal. Within a few years of his death, a casual correspondence with an Episcopal clergyman in England led him into an elaborate discussion of the doctrines of "Original Sin and the Trinity," in which he maintained the views which had been commended to him from the lips of the eloquent Channing, and his able and devoted successor, in the church of which he himself was a faithful and conscientious member. The correspondence reached through twelve long letters, six on each side, — making up a pamphlet of fifty pages; and even those who may differ most widely from his conclusions cannot fail to be struck with the candor, the research, the precision, and the power which he displayed in the argument.

And yet, while Mr. Appleton has left so many evidences of distinguished success in so many varied departments of discussion and controversy, both oral and written, one might hesitate about calling him either a great writer or a great debater. There are, at least, two sorts of persons in the world, — those who cannot tell half they know, and those who can tell a great deal more than they know. The latter sort are generally classed among great debaters and great writers. Mr. Appleton was eminently one of the former class.

He had not the gift of fluent speech. He did not converse easily. He did not communicate with facility or with fulness. "His tongue" (to use the familiar phrase of the Psalmist) was not "the pen of a ready writer." Nor was his pen (if we may reverse that phrase) the tongue of a ready speaker. He made a few invaluable speeches in Congress; but they were laboriously prepared, and gained nothing by the delivery. He wrote, as we have seen, many powerful essays, and a vast number of excellent articles in the public journals: but a dry, terse, unimaginative style characterized them all, without illustration or amplification; and we are continually led to say, as we read them, "What a reserve of information and argument he had! — how much more he knew and felt than he was able to express!" Even his style, however, as far as it went, was a remarkable one, — clear, concise, sententious, pungent, conveying his meaning with marvellous exactness, and singularly adapted to the topics which he treated. Few college-bred men have written purer English. But it was the style of an acute, independent, and often profound thinker, rather than of an attractive writer or an impressive speaker. His productions seem often, indeed, more like the notes of a speech, or the heads of an argument, than like the argument or the speech itself. And so they often were to others, if not to himself. If those who served in Congress, either with him or during his time, from the greatest to the least, could tell from what magazines or reservoirs of fact, experience, and practical knowledge, they derived many of their most effective materials for some of those efforts which won the admiration of their constituents and the country, they would say that it was from the private correspondence, the personal communication, or the published essays of Mr. Nathan Appleton. Nor can we fail to reflect, now that he is no more, what a resource to the National Administration his experience, his sagacity, and his practical wisdom would have been at this moment, in aiding it to provide for the financial exigencies which have resulted from the deplorable conflict into which it has been precipitated by the madness of the Southern States.

He lived long enough to see the commencement of this conflict, and to realize the difficulties, dangers, and momentous issues, which it involved. Conservative and national in all his views, he had always deprecated sectional agitations and contentions, and had combated the course of the Free-soil and Antislavery parties of the North, both by his vote and by his pen; but he had no sympathy with secessionists or disunionists anywhere. His last pamphlet, published as lately as March, 1860, was a letter to his friend Mr. Rives, of Virginia, protesting against the extreme views of the South as well as of the North. And, after the first blow had been struck by Carolina, he knew nothing but his country's cause; and cordially concurred with his political friends in the doctrine, that the Government must be supported, the flag defended, and the authority of the Constitution re-asserted, if possible, over the whole Union. Within a week before his death, he gave his name and a handsome contribution to the reception of a regiment from his native State of

New Hampshire, and regretted that he could not be present to welcome them personally, as they marched through Boston on their way to the defence of the Capital. Yet he regarded the insurrection of the Southern States more in sorrow than in anger, and would have been one of the last to countenance or to encourage the idea of prosecuting the war in any spirit of hatred or revenge, or with any view either of emancipating the slave or subjugating his master.

But the clouds which had gathered so thickly over the country were not the only ones which darkened the closing scenes of the career which has thus been sketched. While the little remnant of his life was to be counted by days, and almost by hours, and while he was awaiting his final summons with calm resignation to the Divine Will, a sudden and most distressing domestic calamity was announced to him, — resulting, after a brief interval, in the death of a beloved daughter, who, in the pride of her matronly beauty, and in the enjoyment of every advantage and distinction which could render her life dear to herself or enviable to others, had fallen a victim to an accident which thrilled the heart of the whole community. "She has gone but a little while before me" was his only response to these startling tidings; and he braced himself up anew to endure whatever his heavenly Father had appointed for him. On the day of her funeral at Cambridge, he rose, and dressed himself in a full suit of mourning, and sat in his accustomed arm-chair, as if he were present (as he was in spirit) at the sad ceremonial. He listened with composure, soon afterwards, to a detailed recital, at his own particular request, of all the circumstances connected with her death and burial, and then retired to his bed for the night. Before another sun had fully risen, his spirit had returned to God who gave it; and, on the third day following, his remains were borne to Mount Auburn, and laid beside the lovely form of his lamented child.

Mr. Appleton has himself referred, in the sketches which have been given, to the death of his first wife in 1833. She had borne him two sons and two daughters. The second son died, of consumption, in 1835. The eldest daughter, who had married a son of the late distinguished English statesman and philosopher, Sir James Mackintosh, and who resides with her husband and children in London, was unable to be with him at the time of his death. The second daughter, the wife of our accomplished and admirable poet, Longfellow, was sadly torn away, as we have seen, while her father was just waiting for his own release. But he had been most happily married again, in 1839, to an amiable and excellent person, by whom he had three other children, who, with their mother and his eldest son, were at hand to watch over his last hours, to sympathize with him under the terrible blow which had fallen upon him and them alike, and to attend him in those closing scenes, for which none less near and dear than wife and children can ever be sufficient.

It would be unjust to Mr. Appleton's character if the impression were to be left that he sunk under the blow which had thus unexpectedly fallen upon him. He had no nervous susceptibilities which exposed him to be prematurely prostrated even by so sudden a shock. The wreaths of oak and ivy which were laid upon his coffin were just emblems of his qualities and career. He was eminently a man of courage and constancy, and had strength of will, and firmness of soul, for whatever event might betide him. But his own days had long been numbered, and the vital flame had so flickered in the socket before the blast of that terrible bereavement reached it, that it was rather a surprise that he had lived so long, than that he had died at last. "I am not afraid," was his reply to a friend who made some suggestion to him only a day or two before this domestic calamity occurred, — "to tell you the truth, I believe I am not afraid of any thing." One of the mottoes which has sometimes been associated with his family arms might peculiarly have been selected as his own motto; and the language in which it has come down to us was by no means unfamiliar to him, — *Ne cede malis, sed contra audentior ito.* If the first half of the line had been adopted in the spirit of a pun upon the family name, (as so many of the old mottoes were,) nothing could have been more applicable to himself personally than the latter half. Partly as the result of physical constitution, and partly as the result of the faith which he had cherished and cultivated through life, he was of a temper never to yield to adversities, but to bear up bravely against them to the end.*

* Another motto of the Appleton Family is *Malis fortiter obsta.* Both breathe the same spirit, and both involve the same play upon words.

Persistent courage and inflexible integrity were, indeed, the two leading elements of Mr. Appleton's character, and constituted the secrets of his great success. To these, more than to any thing else, he owed both his fortune and his fame. He displayed his boldness by embarking in untried enterprises, by advocating unpopular doctrines, by resisting popular prejudices, by confronting the most powerful and accomplished opponents in oral or written argument, and by shrinking from no controversy into which the independent expression of his opinions might lead him. His integrity was manifested, where all the world might read it, in the daily dealings of a long mercantile career, and in the principles which he inculcated in so many forms of moral, commercial, and financial discussion. There is nothing in his "Sketches of Autobiography" more true of himself than the following passage from his memoir of the late Abbott Lawrence, as prepared for this Society in 1856, and published in our Collections: —

"The merchant makes no claim to benevolence or patriotism as his ruling motive in trade: all he professes is absolute and undeviating justice. The morals of trade are of the strictest and purest character. It is not an uncommon opinion, that there is a laxity in the mercantile code, which looks with indulgence on what are called the tricks of trade. It is not so. Whilst the direct object of all trade is gain, individual benefit, not the slightest prevarication or deviation from truth is allowable. There is no class of men with whom the Christian rule, of doing to others what we expect or require in return, is more strictly demanded than amongst merchants. Mercantile honor is as delicate and fragile as that of a woman. It will not bear the slightest stain. The man in trade, who has been found to equivocate or falter in his course, becomes a marked man. He is avoided. It is thus found, by experience, that integrity is almost as uniformly the accompaniment of success, as it always is of character."

It only remains for me to do an act of justice to Mr. Appleton's character, to which he seemed to attach particular importance, and which can best be performed by simply transcribing a memorandum of my own, made at the time. I had called to bid him good-bye before going to Europe, two or three years ago; and found him suffering severely from a racking cough, and hardly expecting to live until my return. After conversing for a few minutes on several topics, in presence of his family, he asked me to go with him into his little private library, where he said substantially as follows: —

"You know I have always told you, that I relied on you to look after my memory after I am gone, and to prepare some little biography or memoir of me, according to the custom of our Historical Society. I have arranged abundant materials, which you shall have at the right time. But there is one point of my character that I do not think the world is in the way of understanding. I have accumulated a large fortune, and people are liable to think that I have been peculiarly devoted to money-making. As I came to Boston a poor boy, this would be a natural inference. Yet nothing is more untrue. The truth is, when I had succeeded in laying up a moderate property, — say two hundred thousand dollars, — I was quite content, and intended to retire altogether from business. It was altogether accidental that I have ever gone further. I have explained something of this in my late pamphlet on the history of Lowell and the Cotton Manufacture. It was wholly accident that I went into that business; and the truth is, that my mind has always been devoted to many other things rather than money-making. That has never been a passion with me, or ever a subject of much concern. Accident, and not effort, has made me a rich man."

Mr. Appleton need have had no such apprehensions as might seem to be implied in these remarks. Neither the employment of his time, his faculties, nor his fortune, had been that of a mere maker or hoarder or lover of money; and no such character could ever have been attached to him by the community in which he lived. The very investment of so large a part of his property in domestic manufactures had many of the best elements of charity; and the satisfaction which he derived from the success by which he was himself enriched, was not a little enhanced by the consideration, that he had been the means of affording employment to so great a number of operatives, of both sexes, who might otherwise have failed to obtain work and wages. But his mind was one of the last that could have contented itself with merely poring over his own day-book and ledger, much as he may have prized the virtues of the trial-balance. He was a person of large reading, diligent study, careful reflection, varied acquisition; whose published writings would alone be sufficient to show how little of his time and thought could have been taken up with any private, pecuniary ends of his own. Harvard University recognized his claims to the distinctions of literature by the honorary degrees of Master of Arts in 1844, and of Doctor of Laws in 1855. The American Academy of Arts and Sciences, the American Antiquarian Society, and other kindred associations, enrolled him among their domestic members; and the Archæological Institute of

Suffolk County, in Old England, placed his name on its foreign honorary list. He had, indeed, accumulated a great estate; but it had brought with it no canker of pride or avarice. He was a liberal, public-spirited gentleman, whose charity began at home, but did not end there; who made handsome provision for a hospitable household and a numerous family, without limiting his benevolence within the range of domestic obligations or personal ties. He was not ostentatious of his bounty, either in life or death; nor did he seek celebrity for his name by any single and signal endowment: but he never looked with indifference on the humane and philanthropic enterprises of the day, nor declined to unite in sustaining those institutions of education and science which are the glory of his time. His sense of justice and his distaste for display prevailed even here; and he preferred being known as "doing his share" in any public cause, to being remarked upon for extraordinary munificence.

The deep interest which he took in our own Society, during a membership of nearly thirty years, has been manifested by his punctual attendance at our meetings, by his frequent donations to our library, and by more than one most timely and liberal contribution to our treasury. His instrumentality was highly effective in our behalf as one of the committee by which our present building was secured to us; and still more as one of the executors of his late excellent brother (Mr. Samuel Appleton) in the establishment of our Publishing Fund, which bears that brother's name. His own name will be cherished in our memories among those which have most adorned our rolls, and will henceforth have a conspicuous place in that list of illustrious Merchants, whose enterprise, integrity, and public spirit have made up so large a part of the best history of Boston.

Mr. APPLETON married, —

First, in 1806, Maria Theresa Gold, eldest daughter of Thomas Gold, Esq., of Pittsfield, who was born 7th November, 1786, and died 10th February, 1833.

Their children were, —

1. Thomas Gold, who was graduated at Harvard University in 1831.
2. Mary, who married Robert James Mackintosh, Esq., formerly Governor-General of the Leeward Islands, and son of the late Sir James Mackintosh, and has issue.
3. Charles Sedgwick, who died 25th October, 1835.
4. Fanny Elizabeth, who married Professor Henry Wadsworth Longfellow, and died (leaving issue) 10th July, 1861.

Mr. Appleton married, second, in 1839, Harriot Coffin Sumner, daughter of Jesse Sumner, Esq., of Boston. Their children are, —

1. William Sumner, who was graduated at Harvard University in 1860.
2. Harriot.
3. Nathan.

The following list of Mr. APPLETON'S WRITINGS is believed to comprise all which have been published in pamphlet form: —

An Examination of the Banking System of Massachusetts, in Reference to the Renewal of the Bank Charters. 1831; pp. 48.

Remarks on Mr. Bouldin's Resolution of Inquiry into the Nature of Minimum Duties. House of Representatives, Jan. 21, 1832; pp. 12.

Speech in Reply to Mr. McDuffie, of South Carolina, on the Tariff. House of Representatives, May 30, 1832; pp. 24.

Speech on the Bill to reduce and otherwise alter the Duties on Imports. House of Representatives, Jan. 23, 1833; pp. 31.

Remarks on Currency and Banking; having Reference to the present Derangement of the Circulating Medium in the United States. 1841; pp. 48 (with Appendix, 73).

Speech on the Tariff and Compromise Act, delivered in the House of Representatives, July 5, 1842; pp. 10.

Labor: its Relations in Europe and the United States compared. 1844; pp. 16.

Correspondence between Nathan Appleton and John G. Palfrey. 1846; pp. 20.

What is a Revenue Standard? and a Review of Secretary Walker's Report on the Tariff. 1846; pp. 23.

Correspondence between Nathan Appleton and John A. Lowell in Relation to the Early History of the City of Lowell. 1848; pp. 19.

Memoir of Hon. Abbott Lawrence; prepared for the Massachusetts Historical Society. 1856; pp. 20.

Remarks on Currency and Banking. Third edition. 1857; pp. 63.

Introduction of Power-loom, and Origin of Lowell. 1858; pp. 36.

The Doctrines of Original Sin and the Trinity; discussed in a Correspondence between a Clergyman of the Episcopal Church in England and a Layman of Boston, U. S. 1859; pp. 50.

Letter to the Hon. William C. Rives, of Virginia, on Slavery and the Union. 1860; pp. 17.

APPENDIX.

MEETING IN THE MERCHANTS' EXCHANGE.

A MEETING of the merchants of Boston was held yesterday, at noon, in the Merchants' Exchange, for the purpose of testifying their respect for the memory of the late Hon. Nathan Appleton. It was attended by a large number of prominent business-men. Mr. J. W. Edmands called the meeting to order; and, after stating the object of the meeting, he introduced Mr. John A. Lowell as the President. Messrs. P. T. Jackson and Israel Lombard were chosen Secretaries.

Mr. LOWELL then made the following remarks: —

I thank you for this nomination. I might have hoped that your choice would have fallen upon some one more used than I to such an office ; and yet I should hardly have been content that this opportunity should not have been afforded me of expressing my appreciation of the public and private merits of Nathan Appleton. No one, perhaps, now living, has been for so long a period intimately associated with him in the pursuits of business ; certainly no one is prepared to render stronger testimony to the sagacity, the public spirit, the unshaken firmness, the high tone of honor, that marked every action of his long and useful career. His name is too intimately connected with finance, with commerce, with all the great industrial pursuits of New England, to need eulogium from any one ; but it is a privilege which we, his fellow-citizens, would not willingly forego, to bear our ready testimony to those qualities which have done more than those of perhaps any other one man to enhance the estimation and promote the prosperity, not of this city only, not of this State, nor of New England, but of the whole of our common country, North, East, West, ay, and South. The time will come, I am assured, when even that now ungrateful and rebellious land will enroll the name of Nathan Appleton among the benefactors our country gave us.

REMARKS OF MR. J. T. STEVENSON.

May I be permitted, Mr. Chairman, to offer a resolution for the consideration of this meeting?

This assembly of so many of our merchants at this unwonted hour, upon the announcement of the departure from the scenes of earth of a gentleman, who, through a long life, has occupied a very prominent position in our commercial community, bears ample testimony to the manner in which his usefulness and virtues have been appreciated here.

Mr. Nathan Appleton was a man fit for an example. He was a loyal and public-spirited citizen, a steadfast friend, a safe adviser, an honorable merchant, and a Christian gentleman. He executed the numerous trusts which his high character in our community enforced upon him, with that scrupulous faithfulness which is the brightest jewel in the ornament of a merchant prince. Notwithstanding his extreme modesty, amounting almost to bashfulness, the intrinsic virtues of his character put him into the front rank of the profession which he had chosen and which he loved. In the conduct of affairs he was very cautious, but truly courageous.

He was a very charitable man; not careless in his bestowments: but rarely did any object which he knew to be a worthy one look for his aid in vain. I have more than once heard him speak, with obvious delight, of the fact, that the ample fortune which his own enterprise had laid the foundations for, and which God had blessed him with, was so invested as to give honorable employment and sufficient wages to large numbers of persons less fortunate in that respect than himself.

He was an accomplished gentleman. Endowed by nature with a vigorous intellect, he had employed his leisure from the active work of business for its cultivation. He studied a subject before he talked about it. He was a logical thinker and a lucid writer. The productions of his pen upon subjects affecting the commercial interests and the political economy of the country have been of marked value.

In his old age, he enjoyed the innocent pleasures of life with a zest that might have become a boy. The lengthening shadows, as his sun went down, cast no obscurity over his mind; but he noted, with the eye of a Christian philosopher, the gradual ebb of his own vital powers. Knowing, as he did, that the time that was lent to him must be measured by only a few days, he approached the confines of eternity, though called upon to bear a terrible domestic burden which an inscrutable Providence had just laid upon him, with unfaltering step. His perfect patience was founded on a firm faith.

I may be asked, "Had our departed friend no faults?" Of course he had, for he was human; and God has not vouchsafed to us that men should be perfect here on earth. But assuredly we may permit the cold hand of death to draw an impenetrable veil over the frailties or the foibles that made our friend a man, while we contemplate the virtues which have fitted him for an angel. May he be an angel to us! Let us imitate his example, and revere his memory; then, though he be sleeping in the grave, he will still be doing good to those who are to follow him.

We have not come here to mourn his loss. He has enjoyed a long and a prosperous life. Twelve years more than "threescore and ten" were allotted to him, and a cheerful spirit prevented old age from becoming a burden to him; and now, in a full maturity, a good citizen, a kind friend, and an honorable merchant, has been gathered to his fathers. But we have come, rather, to bear a cheerful testimony to his large usefulness and to his many virtues.

Permit me to offer the resolutions which I will read: —

Resolved, That the merchants of Boston desire to give expression to their sense of the exalted worth of the Hon. Nathan Appleton, and to testify their respect for his memory.

Resolved, That the character of Mr. Appleton presented an example worthy of imitation; that his vigorous intellect was habitually devoted to useful objects; that his private fortune was so used as to be a public benefaction; that his kind heart, his open hand, his cool judgment, his unswerving integrity, his strict justice, and his pure morality, entitled him to our affectionate respect while he lived, and will prompt us to cherish his memory now that he has gone.

Resolved, That, without intending to intrude upon the sacred sorrow of home, we take this occasion to assure the family of our departed friend of our sincere sympathy with them in their double grief.

Resolved, That, in token of our respect for the deceased, we will attend the funeral services at the King's Chapel this afternoon.

REMARKS OF HON. EDWARD EVERETT.

Mr. EVERETT spoke substantially as follows: —

Mr. Chairman, — I am rather out of place in this hall; but I have cheerfully complied with the request of your Committee in giving my attendance here, to join you in an expression of respect for the memory of Mr. Appleton. It was my happiness to stand in friendly relations to him from my earliest entrance into public life, and to enjoy at all times his political and personal confidence. He was certainly a man of high mark; and he possessed those natural endowments, and traits of character, which would have led to distinction in any walk of life. His career is too well known to those who hear me to need a minute rehearsal. His original inclination seems to have been for a profession. Circumstances, however, led him, after preparing for a collegiate course at Dartmouth, to engage in business; which he pursued, as we all know, for the rest of his life, with intelligence, energy, and success. But he retained to the last his literary tastes, kept up his knowledge of the Latin language, was fond of reading and writing, and gave the public many carefully prepared efforts of his pen. Among these, I may mention his treatise on currency and banking, first published in 1841; a tract on the relations of labor in Europe and America; his account of the introduction of the power-loom into the United States, and of the foundation of the city of Lowell; and his biographical memoir of his friend Mr. Abbott Lawrence, which was prepared at the request of the Massachusetts Historical Society. Mr. Appleton's opinions on the important questions of the day were also occasionally published in the form of letters to his friends; and, a year or two since, an interesting correspondence with an English clergyman on some theological questions was printed by him. All these compositions are marked with clearness of statement, fulness of information, simplicity of style, and vigorous common sense, without any attempt at ornament.

Mr. Appleton entered into business in Boston with his elder brother Samuel in 1795, at the time when the commerce of the United States, under the genial influence of the Federal Constitution, had begun to revive from the paralysis caused by the old confederation. Twelve or thirteen years of prosperity followed, during which he laid the foundations of his fortune. The restrictive system which commenced in 1807 crippled the trade of the country, and gradually forced the thoughts of enterprising men toward manufactures. The first attempts, however, were made without skill or experience, and with imperfect machinery, and did not inspire Mr. Appleton with confidence in their success. Being in Europe in 1811, he met Mr. Francis C. Lowell at Edinburgh, and found that he entertained sanguine hopes, that, through the medium of the power-loom, the cotton manufacture could be introduced into this country. Mr. Appleton was at first less confident; but, when Mr. Lowell — pursuing the object, both in England and after his return, with equal sagacity and perseverance — determined to make the experiment at Waltham, Mr. Appleton cheerfully shared the risk. I need not say to this audience how completely this experiment succeeded. The power-loom was, through the ingenuity of Mr. Lowell, introduced; and many most effective improvements in the spinning machinery were superadded. This success was certainly due, in the first instance, to Mr. F. C. Lowell; and next to him, if I mistake not, to the energy of Mr. Patrick T. Jackson, and the co-operation and influence of Mr. Appleton.

The return of peace and the influx of foreign goods threatened to prostrate our infant manufactures; but they had already acquired a recognized importance as a national interest. Mr. Appleton, in his valuable pamphlet on the subject, informs us (what is otherwise matter of record), that, by the representations of Mr. Lowell, the eminent Southern statesmen, Messrs. Calhoun and Lowndes, were convinced of the expediency of the square-yard duty of six and a quarter cents on imported cottons. These gentlemen were satisfied by Mr. Lowell that they desired no extravagant bounty, but only such protection as would secure them against the fluctuations and gluts of the foreign market. He foretold to them, that, the manufacture once established, the price would be sure to be brought down by domestic competition; and Mr. Appleton's instructive pamphlet shows us, that the goods which in 1816 sold for thirty cents per yard were sold in 1843 for six and a quarter cents per yard, fluctuating from seven to nine cents with the price of cotton. It would be gratifying to know, from those theorists who maintain that a protective duty is, in all cases, added to the price of the domestic article, what would be the price, without the duty of six and a quarter cents, of the article which, with the duty, sells for six and a half cents. If this theory is true (and it is the theory on which South Carolina drove the country to the verge of a civil war in 1832), the price without the duty would be one quarter of one cent per yard!

The success of the enterprise at Waltham led to the foundation of Lowell, in which the name of your kinsman, sir, is so justly commemorated. Mr. Appleton was one of the original proprietors, and engaged a very large capital in the first company. I retain a lively recollection of a visit made there in his company, and that of other distinguished persons (among them Mr. John Quincy Adams), when a single mill only had been built, and the greater part of what is now Lowell lay in a state of nature. The confident expectation was then expressed, that persons at that time living would see it a city of twenty thousand inhabitants. Mr. Appleton himself, though then in middle life, lived to see it a city of forty thousand inhabitants!

But notwithstanding the success of the cotton manufacture at Waltham and Lowell, and many other places in the Northern and Middle States, the protective policy gained friends but slowly. It suffered, in fact, at the hands of injudicious advocates, who desired exorbitant duties, that they might, without capital and without skill, do what required both. Their imprudent demands played into the hands of the Southern politicians, who, for the purposes of local agitation, now made war upon the system which they had themselves aided in building up. Accordingly, when, about ten years after the foundation of Lowell, the question arose, whether this great interest should be sacrificed to the clamors of South Carolina, Mr. Appleton accepted a nomination to Congress as a friend of moderate protection, and was elected as the representative of Boston. I was a member of Congress at the time, and in daily intercourse with him. He was of the class of men that always, at least in quiet times, exercise influence in the House, — men who are not politicians, not office-seekers, not talkers, but who thoroughly understand certain branches of public policy. Mr. Appleton understood manufactures, currency, and banking. He confined himself to these subjects in debate. The House, when he rose, gave him its respectful attention, because they knew, that, though not holding out the attractions of rhetoric, he never spoke without having something to say that was worth hearing.

There was, I suppose, no person in the community who understood the subjects of banking and currency better than Mr. Appleton; few as well. Mr. Webster once, in conversation with me, after mentioning other distinguished financiers, added, "But Mr. Appleton, on these subjects, is our most acute and profound thinker." His tract on currency, first published in 1841, and since reprinted twice, shows, I think, the justice of this remark. I am certainly bound to admit it; for, on one important subject, I must own that he was right, and I was wrong. Sooner than most men, he discovered the false system and dangerous principles on which the Bank of the United States was proceeding, and foretold the crash which afterwards took place. Had every one possessed his discernment in this respect, how much public wrong and private suffering would have been spared!

For the several last years of his life, Mr. Appleton had been withdrawn from active participation in business, beyond what was necessary for the care of his property, of which he made a liberal use as a patron of every meritorious charity and public-spirited enterprise. He watched with patriotic anxiety the progress of our sectional controversies, but took no active part in affairs. I shall not attempt to sketch his private character. Judging from the conclusion of Mr. Stevenson's remarks, which is all I had the good fortune to hear, it is unnecessary to attempt it. I have come not prepared as I could wish, but with these desultory recollections and thoughts, the unstudied dictate of my own feelings, — not a tribute worthy of him, or of the beautiful example which he afforded of a mature, well-balanced character. Eminently happy in his domestic relations, he enjoyed to the full, in the decline of life, so far as impaired health would permit, his well-earned prosperity; moderate in all things, his manners simple and unostentatious, his character spotless, his religious convictions and hopes the governing principle of his life. Mercantile honor he held in all but superstitious estimation. In his memoir of Mr. Lawrence, he says it is a great error to suppose, because the occupation of the trader, from its nature, affords to men of low-toned character a temptation or opportunity for dishonest gain, that therefore the true merchant deems lightly of his honor: "It is as dear to him," he adds, "as a woman's chastity." Of the elevated frame of mind to which he had risen in the last days of his life, the domestic calamity to which Mr. Stevenson has alluded drew out a pathetic illustration. When the intelligence was brought him of the shocking event which destroyed the life of his beloved daughter, he said, "She has only gone a little while before me." We cannot, Mr. Chairman, deeply deplore the close of a life leaving behind it so pure a memory, protracted, as Mr. Stevenson has observed, so far beyond the appointed term, and terminated in a spirit so truly Christian.

I beg leave to second the resolutions which he has laid on the table.

The resolutions were then unanimously adopted; and, on motion of Abbott Lawrence, the secretaries were directed to transmit a copy of them to the family of the deceased.

Mr. Lowell, the chairman, stated that it had been suggested to him, that the merchants of this city close their stores and counting-rooms at four o'clock, that those in their employ might have an opportunity of attending Mr. Appleton's funeral, which was to take place at half-past four o'clock, at King's Chapel. The meeting then adjourned. The above suggestion was quite generally carried out.

The funeral of the Hon. Nathan Appleton took place yesterday afternoon. After the usual services at the late residence of the deceased on Beacon Street, the body was removed to King's Chapel, where a large number of persons had assembled. Among the many distinguished gentlemen present were Hon. Edward Everett, President Felton and Professors Holmes and Lowell of Harvard College, Hon. Robert C. Winthrop, Hon. S. A. Eliot, Amos A. Lawrence, James Lawrence, Abbott Lawrence, and Hon. William Sturgis. The relatives of the deceased were also present. The services were conducted by Rev. Ezra S. Gannett, D.D. After singing by the choir, Dr. Gannett read selections from the King's-Chapel Liturgy, and made an appropriate prayer. After the services, the body was placed in the hearse, and conveyed to the family burial lot in Mount-Auburn Cemetery, followed by a procession of relatives and friends. — *Boston Journal*, 17th July, 1861.

THE MASSACHUSETTS HOSPITAL LIFE INSURANCE COMPANY.

At the stated meeting of the Board of Directors of the Massachusetts Hospital Life Insurance Company, — consisting of the following members: William Amory, Edward Austin, Francis Bacon, J. Ingersoll Bowditch, J. Wiley Edmands, George H. Kuhn, Amos A. Lawrence, Charles G. Loring, Francis C. Lowell, John A. Lowell, George R. Minot, Ignatius Sargent, William Sturgis, — on the seventh day of August, 1861, the following preamble and resolutions were unanimously adopted: —

"The office of President of this institution having been made vacant by the death of the Hon. Nathan Appleton, who, being one of its founders and a director for the space of twenty-six years, has presided over it for the remaining twelve of its existence, and served upon the Committee of Finance throughout both periods, — the members of this Board avail themselves of the opportunity of its first assembling since the event, to express, and place upon record, their profound sense of the value of his services, as among those to whom it is chiefly indebted for its success and usefulness; and to whose extensive knowledge, sound judgment, comprehensive wisdom, and urbane manners, the ease, safety, and pleasure with which its important affairs have been administered, are eminently due; —

"Therefore *Resolved*, That, in the death of the honored head of this institution, the members of this Board lament the departure of an officer most able, efficient, and faithful, to whom they and the other officers of the Company, and all interested in the management of its highly responsible trusts, are deeply indebted for the sagacity, wisdom, and fidelity which he ever contributed in the administration of its affairs; and of a profoundly venerated associate and friend, by whom the labors of all its various departments have been from its foundation enlightened and cheered.

"*Resolved*, That, while thus mourning the removal of an honored officer of this Company and of a revered personal friend, they recognize also the loss, to the city and the commonwealth, of one of their noblest citizens and brightest ornaments; whose extensive knowledge and far-reaching sagacity as a merchant and financier; whose wisdom, patriotism, and magnanimity as a statesman; whose high culture and virtues as a Christian gentleman, neighbor, and friend; and whose spotless and elevating example in all the walks of private and official life, — secured to him the universal love and respect of all who knew him, and should be held in ever-grateful remembrance by those who survive him.

"*Resolved*, That the members of this Board desire individually to express to the family of the deceased their profound sympathy in the affliction attending the departure of one so eminently worthy of all love and respect, however chastened by the reflection that his powers to enjoy and communicate happiness were vouchsafed to a ripe old age, and that neither his virtues nor their influence can ever die; and that Mr. Sturgis and Mr. Loring be a Committee to communicate to them this assurance, together with a copy of these resolutions.

"*Resolved*, That these proceedings be entered at large upon the records of this Company."

A true copy from the records.

Attest: MOSES L. HALE, *Secretary.*

THE MERRIMACK MANUFACTURING COMPANY.

At the adjourned annual meeting of the stockholders of the Merrimack Manufacturing Company, held in Boston, on Wednesday, Sept. 4, 1861, upon motion of Mr. JOHN A. LOWELL, it was unanimously —

"*Resolved*, That the Merrimack Manufacturing Company entertain a high sense of the value of the services of the late Hon. Nathan Appleton, who, for so long a period, contributed to the prosperity of this Company in the varied capacities of selling agent, director, and president. To his sagacity, vigilance, enterprise, and unflinching firmness, should be ascribed, in a large measure, a success to which it would not be easy, in this country, to find a parallel.

"*Resolved*, That the Treasurer be requested to communicate this expression of our deep feeling to the family of Mr. Appleton."

A true copy of record.

Attest: T. P. TENNEY, *Clerk.*

THE BOSTON BANK.

BOSTON BANK, BOSTON, July 15, 1861.

At a special meeting of the Directors of the Boston Bank, held at the banking-room this day, the following expression of the feeling of the members of the Board was unanimously adopted: —

"*Voted*, That the death of the Hon. Nathan Appleton, who has been a director of this bank for more than forty-eight successive years, prompts us to record our appreciation of his great usefulness and of his many virtues.

"Mr. Appleton brought to the performance of his duties here the same faithfulness which characterized his execution of the many important trusts which have been committed to him. The kindness of his heart, the vigor of his intellect, the coolness of his judgment, the strictness of his justice, and the purity of his morals, insured to him the affectionate respect of those who were associated with him during his long and useful life.

"*Voted*, That the Cashier be requested to communicate these proceedings to the family of Mr. Appleton, with an assurance of the sympathy of the members of this Board with them in this hour of their bereavement.

"*Voted*, That this testimonial be entered upon the records of the bank, and that this Board will attend the funeral services in respect to the deceased."

A true copy. JAS. C. WILD, *Cashier*.

STARK MILLS.

At a meeting of the proprietors, held in Manchester, N.H., 26th June, 1861, in consequence of a letter from the Hon. Nathan Appleton, one of the Directors and President of this Company from its first organization in 1838 to the present time, declining a re-election to a membership of the Board of Directors on account of ill health, the following vote was proposed by WILLIAM AMORY, Esq., and passed unanimously; viz.: —

"That this Company receive with great regret the declination of the Hon. Nathan Appleton to remain longer in the Board of Directors on account of ill health; and that the sincere thanks of this Company be tendered to him for the important and valuable services he has rendered so acceptably in his capacity of President and Director, from the organization thereof in 1838 to the present time; and that the Clerk of the Company be requested to present to Mr. Appleton a copy of this vote, with the assurance of the high respect, appreciation, and good wishes entertained for him by this Company, collectively and individually."

Remarks of WILLIAM AMORY, Esq., on proposing a vote of thanks to the Hon. Nathan Appleton: —

Though I am aware, Mr. President, that any remark from any one is superfluous to insure a ready, cordial, and unanimous assent to any vote expressive of personal respect and affection, here or anywhere, for the Hon. Nathan Appleton, or to any grateful expression of our high appreciation of the value of his official services, or of our sincere regret at their loss in this instance, I cannot, in justice to this Company, or to my own feelings, or to the claims of Mr. Appleton, resist the temptation — by a very few words in support of this vote — to put on record official testimony of the estimation in which these services are held by the members, directors, and officers of this Company.

Mr. Appleton has been, as we all know, long deservedly considered, and is often termed, the Father of Lowell; and, if directly less entitled to the same relationship to the city of Manchester, still, as chiefly instrumental in the successful introduction and promotion, by his capital and enterprise, of the manufacture of cotton goods into this country, he may fairly claim, and we proudly concede to him, our filial gratitude and respect as *one* of the Fathers, and among the most influential, liberal, and efficient patrons of this place.

It was especially by the liberal aid of his subscription and example that the first mills in this city were erected, more than twenty years since, by the Stark Company, under an organization appointing him a member of the Board of Directors, and President of the Corporation; and, during the whole of that time, he has uninterruptedly discharged all the duties of that office, with that signal fidelity, punctuality, discretion, intelligence, and kindness for which he has always been distinguished. Rarely, if ever, absent from any meeting of either the Board or the Company, he was always able and ready to aid us with sound, independent, safe, and disinterested counsel.

Boldness tempered with judgment; self-reliance, coupled with a courteous respect for the opinions of others; a rare faculty of generalization, with a minute knowledge of details derived from large and long experience; a hopeful confidence in the character of New-England people and in the progress of New-England manufactures, combined with prudence; a philanthropic interest and sympathy for those employed in our mills, consistent with, and promotive of, the prosperity of the proprietors; a steady, courageous, encouraging defiance of the temporary troubles that interrupt occasionally the success of all business during commercial or political panics and crises; dignity in presiding at our business-meetings, and a genial *bonhomie* at our social entertainments; an example of that directness of purpose and stern integrity which diffuses its influence over the management of every department of any business under his immediate or remote supervision, — such are his claims to our thanks and respects, and our regrets at his resignation.

I omit here, Mr. President, as inappropriate to this occasion, any mention of many other qualities characteristic of Mr. Appleton in private or social life, recognized and respected by his personal friends and the community he belongs to; and confine myself to the enumeration of such only as authorize and enjoin upon us the passage of the vote proposed to express our thanks for the services he has so long and so acceptably rendered, and our regrets that he is compelled by any cause, and especially by ill health, to decline a re-election.

AMERICAN ANTIQUARIAN SOCIETY.

At the Annual Meeting of this Society, held at Worcester on the 21st of October, 1861, the Hon. Levi Lincoln said as follows: —

Mr. President, — The Report of the Council to the Society, which has been read, makes appropriate reference to the recent lamented decease of our late-honored and much-esteemed associate and friend, the Hon. Nathan Appleton, and contains a beautiful and most just tribute to his character. I know not how any thing can well be added to its truthfulness or effect. It was my happiness, personally to have known Mr. Appleton for nearly half a century of years. He belonged to a generation now mostly passed away. There are few of his cotemporaries who survive him; and, of those few, I find myself the only one present here, who may utter the living voice in reverence to his memory.

Mr. Appleton was a man of no ordinary endowments. His liberal, enlarged, comprehensive, and cultivated mind embraced not only the great interests of the community, but the still higher duties of patriotism, and loyal devotion to free institutions and constitutional government. As a legislator and a statesman, he shared largely in the confidence of the people, and was repeatedly honored by official positions in the councils of the State and the Nation. I have myself, sir, had opportunity to witness the untiring labor, the discreet judgment, the signal ability, with which he discharged the public service, and the *commanding influence* which these had upon the action of others. As a member of this Society, we all remember his venerable form; his unfailing attendance, even under the burden of physical infirmity, upon our meetings in Boston; and the various manifestations of his interest in the progress, prosperity, and growing usefulness of our Society. Sir, the Society, in heartfelt sympathy with the Council, in the homage rendered to his virtues by the accepted Report, would doubtless seek to add a distinct expression of its sense of the greatness of the *public loss* in his death; and I ask permission to offer for consideration at this time the following Resolutions: —

"The American Antiquarian Society, since its last meeting, have occasion to deplore, in the decease of the Hon. Nathan Appleton of Boston, the loss of one of its most distinguished and valued members.

"Therefore, to give expression to their sense of the greatness of the bereavement, and of the profound respect in which they hold the character and memory of their deceased associate and friend, —

"*Resolved*, That, in the fellowship of the Hon. Nathan Appleton, this Society enjoyed the countenance, aid, and support of a faithful and attentive member, a devoted friend of scientific research and acquisition, and a munificent public benefactor.

"*Resolved*, That in the public relations which, at different times and for many years, Mr. Appleton sustained to the State and National Governments, as a member of the Legislature of the Commonwealth, and, subsequently, as a representative in the Congress of the United States, his services were eminently distinguished by proofs of untiring assiduity in duty; liberal, comprehensive, and enlightened views of public policy; and a spirit of patriotism commensurate with the principles of the Constitution, and the best interests and honor of the Republic.

"*Resolved*, That, in common with other beneficent institutions with which he was associated; the State which he so long and faithfully served; the business community, to which his whole life was an example of industry, probity, and usefulness, — we mourn his departure, and deeply sympathize with those to whom his death is an irreparable personal affliction.

"*Resolved*, That the foregoing Resolutions be entered at large upon the records of the Society, and a copy thereof be transmitted, by the Secretary, to the Family of the deceased."

www.ingramcontent.com/pod-product-compliance
Lightning Source LLC
LaVergne TN
LVHW011120110826
845150LV00008B/2203